TAKING STOCK

BEING FIFTY IN THE EIGHTIES

CHARLES HANDY

Edited by Brigit Barry

British Broadcasting Corporation

This book is published in conjunction with
a BBC Television series, *Taking Stock: Being fifty in the eighties*

The series is produced by Brigit Barry

Published to accompany a series
of programmes in consultation with the
BBC Continuing Education Advisory Council

© Charles Handy 1983
First Published 1983
Published by the British Broadcasting Corporation
35 Marylebone High Street, London W1M 4AA

This book is set in
10 on 11 point Baskerville Linotype VIP
Typeset by Phoenix Photosetting, Chatham
Printed in England by Mackays of Chatham Limited
Cover printed by
Wood Westworth and Company Limited

ISBN 0 563 16506 5

ONTENTS

Acknowledgment is due to the following:
AUTHOR for ideogram by Y. M. Leung; AUTHOR for extract from *Prime time* by Helen
Franks published by Pan Books; BASIL BLACKWELL PUBLISHERS for extract from *Ageing
for beginners* by Mary Stott; JONATHAN CAPE LTD. for 'The road not taken' from *Collected
poems of Robert Frost*; CONTROLLER OF HER MAJESTY'S STATIONERY OFFICE for extracts
from *Social trends* (HMSO 1981); THE DIRECTOR, NATIONAL INSTITUTE OF ADULT
EDUCATION for extract from Stephen Brookfield's article *Independent adult learning* – in
Volume 13, number 1, 1981; 'Diseases of civilisation'. From Jon Hendricks and C.
Davis Hendricks, *Ageing in mass society; myths and realities* 2nd ed., © 1981, 1977 by
Winthrop Publishers, Inc, Reprinted by permission of Little, Brown and Company;
HARPER & ROW, PUBLISHERS, INC. for extract from *Women of a certain age* by Lillian B.
Rubin; HELP THE AGED for extract from *The time of your life* published by Help the
Aged, in association with the Health Education Council, 1979; MRS. KATHERINE B.
KAVANAGH for extract from *To be dead* by Patrick Kavanagh from *Collected poems*
published by Martin Brian and O'Keefe, 1972; GRANT MCINTYRE LTD. for extract from
The remaking of work by David Clutterbuck and Roy Hill and for extract from *Must
success cost so much?*: P. Evans and P. Bartolome; NATIONAL EXTENSION COLLEGE for
extract from *The unemployment handbook* by G. Dauncey N.E.C. Practical Guide 1981;
PAN BOOKS for extract from *Know your own society* by Michael Fitzgerald, Karen
Margolis & Jock Young; 'Poem for everyman' from *How do you feel?* by John T. Wood
© 1974 by Prentice-Hall, Inc. published by Prentice-Hall, Inc., Englewood Cliffs,
New Jersey 07632; POLICY STUDIES INSTITUTE for 'Facts about the elderly' from *A new
look at the personal social services* P.S.L. Discussion Paper, Feb. 1981 and for extract from
Retirement age and retirement costs by Michael Fogarty published in Policy Studies
Institute Report Dec. 1980; SPHERE BOOKS for the quotations contained in *Tolstoy's
Bicycle* by Jeremy Baker; for extract from THE INSTITUTE OF COMMUNITY STUDIES for extract
from *Loss and change* by Peter Marris published by Routledge and Kegan Paul Ltd; The
following extracts appear by permission of *The Guardian*: 'A wife, who kept her job . . .'
by Jane McLaughlin (29 September, 1981) 'Life and leisure in the third age' by Rita
Sidebottom (24 October, 1981) 'Who gets the job-work' reported by David
Clutterbuck (4 November, 1981).
Acknowledgment is due to the following for permission to reproduce illustrations:
MCGRAW-HILL BOOK COMPANY for the Johari window diagram from *Life work planning*
by Kirn & Kirn, c. 1978; ALLEN R. F. with LINDE S. for chart 'How long will you live?'
from *Lifegain*, 1981. Appleton-Century-Crofts, Norwalk, Connecticut. Reprinted with
permission. J. L. HORN for diagram 'Diseases of civilisation' from '*Psychometric
studies of Ageing and Intelligence*' published in *Genesis and treatment of psychometric
disorders of the elderly* eds. S. Gershon & A. Raskin, (The Raven Press, 1975).

Cover illustration Ellis Nadler
Diagrams by John Gilkes

THE AUTHOR

Professor Charles Handy was born in 1932, the son of an archdeacon in the Church of Ireland.

He had a classical education; when he left University he went to work in Malaysia for an international oil company; later he was an economist in the City of London before returning to academic study for his Master of Science degree at Massachusetts Institute of Technology.

In 1967 he joined the London Graduate School of Business Studies, first as Senior Tutor, then as Professor of Management Development.

In 1977 he was appointed Warden of St. George's House in Windsor Castle; St. George's House has been described as 'a religious think-tank'. During his period as Warden his particular concern was with studies on 'the future of work.'

In 1981, after taking stock of his own life, he chose to become self-employed. Charles Handy is now a freelance writer and consultant to a wide variety of organisations in business, government and the voluntary sector, and a Visiting Professor at the London Business School.

His previous publications are: *Understanding Organisations* and *Gods of Management*.

Professor Handy is married with two teenage children.

AUTHOR'S ACKNOWLEDGMENTS

This book would not have been possible without the help of very many people. Brigit Barry of the BBC conceived commissioned and edited the book and has been guide philosopher and friend throughout. She sought out many of the experts in the territory covered in the book and canvassed their views, particularly Audrey Collin, Dr Michael Fogarty, Dr Irene Gore, Professor Alastair Heron, Dr Malcolm Johnson, Professor H. A. Jones, Professor David Metcalfe, Sheila Rothwell and Douglas Woodhouse.

I am most grateful for the chance to be privy to the thinking of these people although they should not, of course, be held responsible for any of what actually appears in the book.

I am also grateful to the many men and women around the country who agreed to take part in discussion groups about the book and this subject, and to David Newell and Vicki Moore who organised the discussions.

Brigit, John, Vicki and Maggie of BBC Education have greatly enriched the book with their ideas, comments and suggestions. Without their diligent and detailed vetting, the book would not be the half of what it is, while without Suzy's unceasing efforts on my behalf it would never have reached book form.

I am also indebted to those individuals who allowed me to quote from their letters or from their published work and to the many publishers who gave me permission to reprint excerpts from their works.

CHARLES HANDY

CHAPTER ONE

THE NEW QUESTIONS

I am fifty this year. When I was twenty it seemed impossible that I would ever be that old. If I survive that long, I felt, I will at least have got everything sorted out, the world will have settled down and there will be time to reap the harvest of my life in secure stability. It doesn't seem like that today, for to be fifty in the eighties looks like being a new experience, not quite like anything that has happened before, with a set of new questions to which there are no old answers. The game has changed.

None of us are strangers to change. The last fifty years have seen enough technical and social changes to confound any forecaster. Who in the early thirties was predicting Jumbo jet aircraft, video-recorders, CB Radio, the Pill, space shuttles, or a one in four divorce rate? If they did predict it, who believed them? Yet, we have survived, most of us, taking change in our stride. The capacity of human beings to survive quite cataclysmic change is always astonishing. To talk to the victims of revolutions, to the survivors of natural disasters, to the children growing up in Northern Ireland, is to be amazed by their resilience, by how life goes on for them in spite of everything.

Cataclysm is certainly on the cards for the eighties. Nuclear war, a clash between the nations of the north and the south, civil war between the rich and the poor in our own land, the prospect of increasing poverty, and of a land supported by robots – these are enough to frighten anyone.

It is right to be worried about cataclysm. It is also right to do whatever we can to prevent it. At the same time, ordinary life has to go on. We cannot and do not plan for cataclysm in our daily lives with the ironical result that the things which concern us most, as we look at the next ten years, are smaller, more local and, at first sight, more inconsequential than the items which top the world's agenda.

We have to live life on two levels. A fifteen-year-old in America was asked to produce a list of the kinds of critical events she saw looming up in the future. It went like this:

A US/USSR alliance against China
A cancer cure
Test-tube babies
An accidental nuclear explosion
Spread of anarchy throughout the world
Robots holding political office in the United States

When she was asked to produce a similar list of critical events for her own personal life, she wrote down:

Moving into my own apartment
Interior design school
Driver's licence
Getting a dog
Marriage
Having children
Death

Life's like that – a mixture of the cosmic and the commonplace, for the fifteen-year-old in America and the fifty-year-old in Britain in the eighties, but the two sets of critical events are unlikely to be quite so separate for the fifty-year-old who cannot escape the inexorable pressures of economics, of technology, and of a changing population structure. This book is about the big and the small, but it is not about cataclysm. That needs another book and there are many of them. I am assuming, sometimes more from hope than from conviction, that the world will go on. The image I have is of sunlight shining through a wood. As I look at the decade ahead, I can see glimpses of great possibilities, gleams of new opportunities and the hint of a new kind of society and better ways of life for all of us. But the wood gets in the way of the sunshine. There are all the obstacles thrown up by our own institutions, by the systems which society has devised to hold itself together, by our own expectations of what is owed to us and what success means, and most of all, by our reluctance to get into that wood and march towards the sunshine at the other side. The Chinese put it another way. They combine the signs for danger and opportunity to give them the ideogram of crisis.

We can look into an uncertain future and see it as a problem and a threat, cursing a world which changed the rules of the game just when we had learned how to play it, or we can see uncertainty as a blank page on which to write our own script.

I have tried in this book to look at some of the dangers and opportunities that are around and to put them into conceptual groups or frameworks, so that we can the better 'take stock' of them and not be mesmerised by them. They come out then as sets of questions to which we must provide answers, as individuals with our own lives to lead, and as citizens with some responsibility for shaping society for those who come after. People in their fifties, whatever their rôle or position in life, and however self-effacing or humble they may be, have to accept that they are likely to have a bigger share than most in whatever power and influence and general clout there is around. We cannot get out of the leadership rôle, in our own bits of the world, even if we want to. We have to lead the way into the future, and find new answers to new questions. I have my own answers to these new questions but my answers need not be anyone else's answers. We have each to find our own way into the future, and the book does provide some 'hints for travellers' – but there can be no sure map to so much unexplored territory.

THE BIG QUESTIONS

There are three questions which run through the book and keep demanding an answer. No-one in their fifties can really escape from them and the answers we each give will affect our lives.

1 How big is the change?

Do we stand on a 'hinge of time' so that many things, like work, the family, or prosperity, will never be as they used to be, or are we only experiencing a small hiccup in the steady progress of society? Should we, as individuals, sit it out for a year or two or must we start to rethink our priorities?

2 Is there a Third Age?

Can we look forward, unlike our parents, to two decades of active life beyond employment and beyond parenthood? Some have called this the Third Age to distinguish it from retirement. If there is this new period in life, because we live longer and cease work earlier, what are we going to do with it? In our fifties we are on the edge of this Third Age.

3 Do we need new rules in society?

If there is a changed world with more people living in this Third Age will we need to adjust some of our laws and regulations to make sure that the new society is a *fair* society for all its citizens? If so, what should we, as individuals and as citizens, do about it? We, after all, will be the first to experience the consequences of the first two questions. Our experience and our feelings of what is fair have to be important.

> I asked several people to tell me their thoughts on where society was going.
> One of them, Ronald Eyre, replied
> 'The questions "What society do I want?" and "What society are we heading for?" aren't very real to me and I'd feel false trying to answer them.
> '"Where are we?" and "What elbow room is there?" seems a bit nearer the point. And halfway through "Where are we?" I start to wonder who "we" are. Apart from using the same drainage and water-supply and sharing a whiff of euphoria when the tube fares come down or there are fireworks in Hyde Park, I don't think of my fellow-Londoners and me as "we" at all; though after a trip elsewhere – especially to the country – I do recognise that "we" look in general rather puzzled and ill and can't be doing ourselves any good living in this city. But here's where we are.
> 'You can talk at the moment about "the imminent collapse of this society" and many people will know what you mean.
> 'A High Court Judge in a lunch break from the Old Bailey told me gloomily over his avocado and prawns (this isn't an ambiance I'm used to) that society wasn't going to collapse – it had collapsed already.
> 'It's sometimes hard to point out that, by analogy with a collapsed wall, some sorts of life flourish for the time being fairly well in rubble. The few experiments in communal living I've come across seem to be under fewer pressures now than they might be if we lived under some religious or political orthodoxy. And what they are discovering may be important for a bit of the future.
> 'Naturally, when mass religion returns or a Great Dictator is invited to tidy up the mess, there may well be general relief. The people who live in nooks and crannies are then going to have to look out, but for the time being we seem to have a little elbow room. It's best not to boast about it because it's fragile. On the other hand you can't deny it's there.'

Early on, I had to face the issue of whether these questions would require different responses for men and for women. As I listened to people in their fifties it became more and more striking to me, that, *at this stage in life*, there was going to be much more that was similar than was different between the two sexes. Of course, each sex typically

10

reaches the fifties by a different route, with a different set of experiences, each with different memories to build on, different things to unlearn; but from now on, the rôles, attitudes, and life-styles seem to come together in a remarkable way, partly because of the answers to the first two questions. Men may have more unlearning to do while women may be more accustomed to the life that is coming up, which may explain why most of the problems are directed at men. All this may, however, be the man in me speaking. If that is so, then I can only recommend that those women who feel that their specifically female problems are not addressed should turn for additional reading to some of the excellent books on the topic of mid-life which have been written by women for women, two of which are listed in Chapter 9.

THE FIRST QUESTION – A HINGE OF TIME?

Are things really changing?

We cling to the familiar because we find security in what we know, and may even prefer the bad old days to the promise of new good days if the new days have to be very different. It is only when change comes in familiar rhythms that we can take it, so that the changing seasons are no threat, quite the reverse, and the seasons of a man's life are rhythmic too, even if we want to speed up the rhythm when we are children and slow it down as we grow older.

It is understandable, therefore, if people resist the idea that there is anything special about being fifty in the eighties.

To be fifty is part of rhythmical change. We know about it and can anticipate it and have experienced it at second-hand in our parents. 'To be fifty is to be forty only more so', someone told me. The idea then that society is at the same time changing around us is just an unwanted complication. We will be more comfortable if we deny it as long as we can, carefully directing our gaze at the familiar – avoiding any evidence of new ways. What, however, is the truth? Is there anything radically different about being in one's fifties today? Do we, as I think, stand on a hinge of time in this country, watching and feeling (because hinges can hurt) a door closing on old ways and opening on new scenes?

Consider for a moment the generation which is now in its fifties – the cohort of the 1920s, as sociologists would describe them. We had experiences which were unique to us in our time and which have shaped our expectations. We reached adulthood at the time the Welfare State was born in the middle and late fifties, and have lived our working lives in a time of constant economic growth and full employment which was a pleasant contrast with childhood memories of depression. Every cohort is different. This was the one which 'never had it so good' in our thirties and forties. Can it continue that way in our fifties?

Many people don't think so. The oil price-hikes in the 1970s, clobbered, for a generation at least, the idea of continually growing economies everywhere, with the contest being only who grows faster than whom. In time, perhaps, new sources of energy will again dramatically lower the price of the fuel of growth but not in time for us. Many of the things we need in life can now be made more cheaply in the developing and newly-industrialised countries, whilst the things we still make ourselves are often better, and more cheaply, made by machines than by people. That scenario suggests that we have, firstly, got to find new ways of earning money abroad. Secondly, it implies that there will be fewer jobs in factories, and perhaps offices, than we are accustomed to.

These possibilities will be examined in more detail later in the book but they add up to a probability, if not a certainty, that the escalator of prosperity for the cohort in their fifties has stopped.

This affects the work we do, for one thing. I took it for granted that my conventional career would continue through until my mid-sixties. Some time ago that began to look very unlikely. It is now clear, as I shall argue in the next chapter, that there are not going to be enough conventional jobs for all who want them, which almost certainly means that we shall see many more unconventional jobs with more people in self-employment, working part-time, working from home or in the near neighbourhood.

More unconventional work will mean money problems for some. It will also make it harder to separate work from the rest of life, and will make nonsense of some of the categories we use at present to define oneself in today's society; more men will discover what many women have long known, namely, how hard it is to fill in that space in one's passport for occupation with one word when one really needs to write a paragraph. Words like unemployment, retirement, and redundancy only have meaning in the context of paid employment. Self-employed people are not allowed to register as unemployed, nor does one think of housewives as ever retiring or of a farmer being redundant. It may be good that these demeaning words are used rather less, but they all have supportive measures that go with them. We shall need new means of support to go with new conventions about work.

What new work there is in paid employment will be at least as well-suited for women as men. Horny-handed sons of toil will be needed less and less. Most work will be white-collar or white coat, as the Irish are finding with their new development industries, work which often appeals less to the man than to his wife.

12

Will we then find house-husbands becoming as common as house-wives? The new technology which makes complicated things simple and large things small will give us tools which even the most incompetent of us can use to make things and do things, from home maintenance to teaching, which previously we had to pay others to do for us. Does this mean that everyone can create a mini-factory in his garden shed? But what, then, do you do if you live in a high-rise block and have no shed? Perhaps you can 'telecommute' from your office in the living-room. All of this suggests that it may no longer be so easy to put work and leisure in separate boxes, or to get all your money out of one box. Work, of a sort, could go on in retirement.

But what will we be working for? For a more prosperous materialist Britain? Maybe not. Enough, many people seem to be saying, is enough, and more than enough is not worth the effort. Recent surveys suggest that Britons, more than other people, prefer a quiet life to a prosperous one. But who then will pay for all those who have left employment or have not saved for it and still need money to live on? Does a quiet life mean less for all, and if so do we really want it? Many people who talked to me felt that materialism had been exhausted and that we were missing the spiritual element in life. Will this come back in some form?

In a poll carried out for *The Times* in June 1980; 60% of middle class correspondents (compared with 43% from the working classes) said that they would not work longer hours for more money; 61.5% said that they had no ambition to earn more than their present earnings. Can it be that the middle classes are already beginning to trade time against money? They it were who developed the work ethic that produced the Industrial Revolution. Are they now evolving a broader ethic more appropriate to the society which is coming?

There are some to whom all these questions are 'little local difficulties' which could be tidied up by a better or at least a different government. To most of the people in their fifties, however, to whom I listened, there were signs of a radically different scene emerging about which government could do little. Society was moving on its hinges, some were going to be squeezed, some would be excited, some depressed, all would be affected. These people who were talking were ordinary men and women working, or occasionally, not working, in places such as Romford, Wolverhampton, and Doncaster. They did not expect to starve or, most of them, to die in any nuclear holocaust. They knew, too, that barring accidents, most of them were going to live for another thirty years. They wondered, in a mixture of curiosity, anxiety, and some excitement, what sort of world it was they would be living in.

'People have been telling us for years and years that the hours of work are going to get less and less, and the years of work are going to get less and less. They've been telling us this for twenty years, but no-one has done anything about it. No-one has told us what we can do instead.'

'The message which I get is that you are chucked off after 50. This is as far as you can go. Nobody wants you. You're on the way out as far as work is concerned.'

'This day has been coming for thirty years. Now I'm not against change and I thought that when I got older I would drop into a nice little job and let younger men have the aggro. But it hasn't worked out like that.'

THE SECOND QUESTION – THE THIRD AGE?

To be in your fifties in the 1980s is to be part of a new experience in another way too. Society is only just beginning to wake up to the fact that, for the first time, a whole generation is entering the sixth decade of life with a good expectation that there will be a third slice of life ahead of them, different from all that went before. The French talk of the three ages of man, the ages of growing, of working, and of living. They are wiser in their traditions than the British who used to say 'born a man, died a baker', implying that one's work filled the whole of life. Indeed, until recently, the pension fund of one company (in America) had the dubious record of only paying out a pension for an average of three months for each individual before they died.

Today, however, all of us can contemplate a full 'Third Age'. We will, on average, live on well into our seventies and many will go to eighty, ninety, or even beyond. The Japanese are planning for an average hundred-year life in the next century.

At the same time as life is stretching out, work is shrinking. We used to plan on working until sixty-five but already one third of the sixty to sixty-five age group is retired and the percentage is rising fast. Many retire before sixty and have not yet come into the statistics (which are always a step behind the social changes). Add to these those who are unemployed and those who choose not to register and it is clear that our working life is ending sooner than it used to.

A gap is opening up between the end of employment and the end of life. The gap may be as big as thirty years for some, but will be fifteen or more for most of us. They need not be years of illness for, as a later chapter points out, medical science has banished most of the infectious diseases which used to kill us in spite of ourselves. Today the things that kill us before time itself gets hold of us are the so-called 'diseases of civilisation' which we inflict on ourselves through stress, cigarettes, and alcohol, amongst other things.

14

We can today choose to stop killing ourselves. The Third Age can then be twenty to thirty years of active life, starting around fifty and ending in the seventies or later.

Death, for nearly everyone, now happens well after seventy. In 1880 a woman of fifty could not expect to make it into her seventies whereas now, on average, she will live another twenty-nine years until she is seventy-nine. Men aged fifty can now confidently expect to live until they are seventy-four, whereas in 1880 it would have been sixty-eight, one or two years after retirement – if they did get as far as retiring. There was no Third Age for men, and only a short one for women.

What can we do with this Third Age?

The answer to our first question suggests that there won't be many conventional jobs available. But that does not mean that there should be no work. There is no need to see the Third Age as a life-sentence to endless television or gardening. It can be the time to put forgotten and unused competences to work, *if* we can learn how to organise ourselves. Without office or factory, men can too easily drift into inertia. Women have more skill and experience in organising themselves to make something happen. Indeed, one feature of the Third Age may be that the rôles and lifestyles of men and women become much more similar. It is the men, however, who will have the more difficult transition to make.

The Third Age – Undiscovered Competences

Did you know that:

Ronald Colman and Cary Grant were both fathers for the first time in their fifties

Winston Churchill was Prime Minister for the first time at sixty-five

Magnus Pike got the Best Television Newcomer Award at sixty-six

Havergal Brian composed his first symphony at eighty, and seventeen more before his death at ninety-three

Roy Thompson bought *The Times* at seventy-two and moved his company into the North Sea Oil industry when he was seventy-seven

Charlie Coles cycled fifty miles in two hours twenty-one minutes aged seventy

Claude Pepper became a Congressman in the United States for the first time at sixty-two and sponsored legislation forbidding the US government to have any fixed retirement age

Quoted by Jeremy Baker in *Life Patterns*

Perhaps more of our energies in the Third Age will go into relationships. Families are spreading out vertically rather than horizontally. Anyone in their fifties today is likely to have both parents and children alive and independent. They may well find themselves still children but also grandparents. Divorce, we know, may ruin families, but it can also result in a child having four parents. With four parents, four grandparents, four step grandparents and maybe six or seven great-grandparents, who needs aunts and cousins? The family is not dead, by all accounts, just growing in a different way. Again, people in their fifties are in the thick of it. And if the new-look society means that we will spend more of our time at or around home, then families, neighbours, and local friends will become more important, substituting a little for the so-called 'community of work'.

Because we have fewer children on average than our parents did we encounter the 'empty nest' situation sooner, when the last of the children leaves home to get married. Today that happens to many mothers in their late forties or early fifties, bringing with it the obvious sense of loss but also the reality of freedom. The emptying nest is the herald of the Third Age. Can we live up to the opportunities offered by this new freedom?

In 1981 a University of the Third Age was started in Britain. It is an outward and visible sign of a new population with new educational needs. The Third Age is alive and well and living in Britain. We in our fifties will soon be entering it if we have not already done so. It is timely to start thinking about it and planning for it before we leave the second age of full-time work or permanent responsibility.

We probably won't think about it, however, unless we are forced to.

'Challenges are something I can easily do without.' That comment by a steelworker facing redundancy could be echoed by many. The invitation to rethink one's life, even for the benefit of one's grand-children, is more than a bit threatening, and most of us are far too humble to want to think of creating a fashion. 'I take each day as it comes', said another, 'and try to enjoy it.' He was explaining why he was reluctant to think about the Third Age of life but was at the same time demonstrating that he had already arrived at a way of living it.

Few of us sit down and decide to rethink the rest of our lives. Schools for life-planning or self-awareness are more common in Los Angeles than in Doncaster or Wolverhampton. But rethinking is often forced upon us by a trigger event. It can happen when one has one's first close acquaintance with death. The effect is to make you realise, in your gut, that you too will die one day. Death is no longer a statistical logical event but a real one. Anyone who has been dangerously ill in hospital will know what this means. To others it can happen when a

16

parent dies – a major structure in one's life, often unappreciated at the time, is gone, death is real and will happen to us too. This taking-on-board of death happens to most people in their forties or early fifties – younger people cannot really understand the emotions it arouses. There is first some quite natural depression, which is usually followed by relief – 'Now I know where I stand, how long I've got; now I can be realistic about what I can achieve'. The result for some is a kind of happy resignation, while for others a new source of energy is released. There are other trigger events: divorce, redundancy, the marriage of the children, the menopause. These all remind us that some chapter of our life is closed, that the page has to be turned and a new chapter started. We cannot continue exactly as before.

I hope that this book may help some people to find new paths to follow if and when the old ones come to a dead end, or no longer satisfy us.

Robert Frost captured the challenge and the opportunity of the Third Age in this poem:

The Road Not Taken
Two roads diverged in a yellow wood,
And sorry I could not travel both
And be one traveler, long I stood
And looked down one as far as I could
To where it bent in the undergrowth;

Then took the other, as just as fair,
And having perhaps the better claim,
Because it was grassy and wanted wear;
Though as for that the passing there
Had worn them really about the same,

And both that morning equally lay
In leaves no step had trodden black.
Oh, I kept the first for another day!
Yet knowing how way leads on to way,
I doubted if I should ever come back.

I shall be telling this with a sigh
Somewhere ages and ages hence:
Two roads diverged in a wood, and I –
I took the one less traveled by,
And that has made all the difference.

THIRD QUESTION – NEW RULES FOR SOCIETY?

If I am right and society is experiencing a major social change we cannot sit idly by, cultivating our roses or learning Swahili. The younger generation see us as creating the world they will inherit. We may feel,

17

individually, powerless, but we have at least the ability to take a view on the way the rules should be, or to express that view in some sort of action, even if it is only to nudge our chosen local politicians in the right direction. The Third Age is not an invitation to escapism.

Society today is programmed for growth and for work; understandably, because social justice is much easier when there is more every year to go round. Cake-splitting is less acrimonious if the slices are larger, even if some are still larger than others. Stop the growth and the argument swells, for now my larger piece of cake has to mean a smaller one for someone else. That can be a recipe for a nasty society if we are not careful, a society where those who have it hold on to it and even increase it, at the expense of those who have not. Does a just world mean a world where everyone gets what he *deserves* by way of reward or of punishment; where hard work is rewarded by profit? Or does a just world mean one in which everyone gets what he *needs*, and the poor need more than the rich? Growth allowed some opportunity for both views to flourish. No growth means that there has to be conflict between them, a conflict already apparent as the two political parties which correspond to these two views of justice move more to the extremes. Practical justice has to be a balance.

Compromise is essential in a democracy, as I shall argue in a later chapter, but the process of hammering out new compromises based on new assumptions about growth is going to preoccupy us in the 1980s. I shall be listing some of the key areas and pointing to the scope for possible compromises. As citizens, particularly as leading citizens in our own worlds, we need to take a view in a decade which will be ferociously political, because the answer to 'What is fair?' is never a logical, rational one, but always a political one.

Let us take just one example of future acrimony.

Society has always found it convenient to use work as the way to push money around. Money is the means to most of what we need in life. The demands for goods, expressed as purchasing power, starts the economic engine; if the consumers have no money, no goods are produced. But how do they get the money in the first place? By payment for their work, or in the case of pensions, payment for their past work, and since most households have one or more people working the coverage is almost perfect; everyone has access to some earned money and through it, to the goodies which society offers. What, then, happens if there is not enough work available at the right level to give every household a livelihood, or the means to live? Traditionally, needy households are given money to tide them over, through unemployment pay or supplementary benefits. If this temporary condition becomes permanent, however, then we are accepting the principle of a citizen's wage, the right of everyone to a basic income, whether he works or not. Is this fair? What alternative is there? Let them starve? Not since Tudor times has that been a possible solution. Provide them with goods and services, not cash, when they need them? Then we are indeed in a 'command' economy telling us how we should eat, drink and sleep. It is an unsolved dilemma because all politicians hope that the jobs will come back. As I will argue, there is no way in which *enough* conventional jobs can come back.

The slow collapse of work raises big questions about who pays for whom, how the available health and education facilities, for instance, should be allocated (to those who need them or those who can afford them?) and how taxes should be collected (from those who work or from those who spend?). These are all questions of fairness. So is the problem of pensions which are rapidly becoming a charge upon our successors as the funds we thought we were building up fail to keep up with inflation and inflated expectations. Is it fair to make your successors responsible for keeping you in the style of life you became accustomed to while you were working?

There are no clear answers, but at least the questions can be put and the options discussed, which is what I shall be doing, particularly in the last chapter.

Throughout this book I shall emphasise the need for positive thinking, the necessity to keep one's eyes on the sunshine in spite of the thickness of the wood. There is, however, no avoiding the lessons and the warnings in history of what to expect when growth disappears and there is major structural change. Greed, self-interest, and violence in defence of one's own become commonplace.

In Britain that could mean bitter warfare between the classes, the races, the rich and the poor, between north and south, the managers and the workers, the paid and the unpaid. If those of us who are entering on the Third Age want to enjoy it, we have to find the right rules for a changed society, which is why this third question and the last chapter of this book may be the most important of them all, even though there is space only to headline the principle problems. Each of us, powerless though we may feel, can contribute to changing that society. I like to remind myself of the story told by the novelist Jean Giono of the man who planted acorns.

The man who planted acorns

Jean Giono tells how in 1913 he was walking in the lonely desolate area of the Vaucluse in the South of France which in those days was a high upland area covered only by sparse scrub and battered by shrill winds. No crops grew there and few people. It was barren and foresaken.

One evening, as dark fell, he found himself far from any village and

Cont.

sought shelter for the night in a shepherd's cottage. The shepherd, a man of some fifty years, said little but gave him a bed. In the morning, as Jean Giono watched, the shepherd counted out, from a bag, one hundred acorns, and then, taking with him a long metal rod, went out to look for his sheep. Jean Giono walked with him and saw how every yard he dug his rod into the ground and dropped in an acorn. Yes, he said, he did this every day. That way he planted over thirty thousand acorns a year of which some ten thousand survived and grew into small oak trees. Look, he pointed, you can see now the ones I planted four years ago when I started.

Next year the World War started. When Jean Giono next visited the area in 1919, there was a forest of small saplings that stretched for five kilometres. Each year it grew, and each year Jean Giono returned. In 1930, many of the trees were three times as high as a man, and the small forest stretched for eleven kilometres. In the mid-thirties, the authorities in Paris discovered this 'maiden' forest, and announced it as the first spontaneous forest known to modern man. They appointed a forest ranger to look after it but the shepherd went on tending his sheep at the edges and planting as he tended.

In 1947, after yet another World War, the shepherd died in a home for elderly folk in Nîmes. Today that region is alive with streams and crops and villages. Ten thousand people live in a place where only wild animals used to roam, for the forest has tamed the climate and made it beautiful. It is a marvellous work of creation by one man, unknown, unthanked, who in his way changed the world a little each day.

CHAPTER TWO

WHAT WILL THE EIGHTIES BE LIKE?

People are puzzled, apprehensive, curious.

'It won't be the same again.'

'Our experience is based on the past and the past is no longer relevant.'

'Why don't they tell us what is going on?'

Prophecy is a dangerous profession. No-one can be sure of what is going to come out of a period of change. But we are already in the thick of the eighties and some trends are becoming clear. What we do with them is another matter. We don't have to let the possible become the inevitable in society or in our lives. This chapter will look at what is going on so that we can see more clearly what options are open to us and what needs to be done.

THE THREE ECONOMIES

To understand what is going on it may help to start with a simplified description of what is happening to the economy of the country. Are we really getting poorer or not? Who is supplying whom and how? Who is paying for what?

It helps to think of the country as having three 'economies' working inside it. An 'economy' is a set of activities which in some way or other add value to the world.

The **Market Economy** is the easiest to see, because that economy consists of all the businesses whose job it is to make things or to provide services for money to those who want them. Factories, shops, banks, and launderettes, are clearly in the market economy, but private schools, the private medical sector, and the churches, are businesses of a sort also; so are British Gas and British Telecom. It does not matter, for the purpose of this analysis, who owns the businesses in the market economy. Nationalised or not, they are there to do things for people who are prepared to pay for them. They also have to earn our foreign exchange to pay for the things we need to import. Out of their income they pay taxes. Some of those taxes are collected on their profits, but most are collected from the wages and salaries of people who work for them (income tax and national insurance) or from the prices of the products (VAT and duty). This tax principally goes to pay for:

The **Redistribution Economy** which is essentially the state sector. I have called it the redistribution economy to make the point that what it is doing is redistributing the wealth collected from the market economy in services like the police, hospitals, schools, roads, local government. It does not charge for these services with the result that these are all forms of income to each of us, an income which is paid in kind, not in cash. There are also some cash payments, like pensions, social benefit and unemployment pay.

The redistribution economy can, in theory, be only as big as the market economy can pay for, and if taxes in that economy are raised too high, everyone shrieks. In practice, all governments borrow. In effect, they borrow from our grandchildren, by running up deficits and debts which their successors will inherit. There is, again, a practical limit to how far they can do this, and most governments quickly come up against this limit when the interest rates or inflation rates get too high.

The redistribution and market economies together make up the formal economy, the one that gets counted. All the activities in these economies added together make up the economic output of the country, whether these activities are policing or selling toys in Regent Street.

It isn't quite as simple as that, of course. Some of the money the government needs to pay for the redistribution economy comes from the taxes paid by the people who work in the redistribution economy. If the government therefore cuts the numbers employed, it cuts its costs but also a bit of its income. The redistribution economy is also the biggest customer through its hospitals, schools, offices, etc., of the market economy, so that, once again, if the government cuts the expenditure of the redistribution economy, it also cuts the income going to the market economy and therefore some of its own income. It's a sort of Catch 22 situation.

But there is a third uncounted economy which adds to the confusion. This is the **Informal Economy**. It has three parts, the black economy, the household economy, and the voluntary economy.

In the informal economy, we make things, grow things, cook things, wash things, and repair things for ourselves, and for others, but because we, usually, charge no money for them they don't get counted or taxed, or included in the calculations of national wealth. Housework, home decorating, plumbing, and gardening, are the most obvious examples of work in this economy. People from time to time estimate the financial value of housework (the latest figure was £210 per week) and there is an old economist's joke that if all married men employed each other's wives as housekeepers (so that the same money flowed in and out) the economy would appear to grow by five per cent, because the activity would then be part of the market economy and so would be counted even though exactly the same work was being done as had been done before.

Actually, some of the work in the informal economy does get charged for – the work which goes on in the *black* or hidden economy. This is work which really belongs in the market economy but because no-one declares it, it does not get counted (or taxed). It may be as large as seven per cent of the two formal economies combined. It goes on everywhere. In Italy it may be as large as twenty per cent of the formal economy, in Russia perhaps more than that. No-one quite knows, for obvious reasons. Governments, quite naturally, would like to pull this business activity into the open, into the formal market economy, because they could then collect taxes from it. Those who work in the black economy as well as those who buy from it are less eager to have it recognised because it would cease to be such a bargain for both parties.

Larger, however, than the black economy is the *household* economy. This is the main part of the informal economy – it includes cooking, gardening, DIY work. It has been estimated that in the United States this uncounted work could be equivalent to half of all the labour costs in the formal economy if it was charged for properly. In primitive societies, the household or home economy is obviously going to be much more than half. It might well be more than half in Britain because the British are particularly inclined to do things for themselves if they possibly can. The British are more likely than most nations to ask you home for a meal rather than take you out to a restaurant. It would be much better for the visible economy, of course, if they did take you out to the restaurant, because more money would then change hands producing more taxable revenue and more opportunity for the employment of cooks and waiters. Whether the food would be so good is another matter.

Two generations ago clothes were washed on a scrubbing board at the kitchen sink. One generation ago, they were sent out to a laundry or launderette. This introduced a new activity to the market economy. Money changed hands and was counted and taxed. People were employed. It was called 'economic growth' and the country visibly grew richer even though the same clothes were washed as were washed before.

Today most homes have a washing machine and clothes once again get washed at home. The initial purchase of the machine, a little soap powder and some electricity is all that gets counted by economists. The country seems to have got a little poorer, and laundries close down, but the same clothes get washed as got washed before.

Music is another example. We used to make music around the fireside, with fiddles and pianos and voices. Then music was made for us in the recording studios and a business was created. Today more and more kids tape their music from the radio, legally or illegally. The amount of money in the music business may get less but more music may be made.

Speculating just a little, we can observe that forty years ago people serviced their own cars. Then service stations sprang up to do it for them and a new business was created. New technology may well make it possible for us to service our own cars again before too long, using very sophisticated new equipment which we buy with the car, if indeed they need servicing at all. Service stations will then disappear and part of a business will die but cars will still get serviced. Are we richer or poorer?

Economists and governments know as well as anyone that there is a lot of work and business going on which never gets counted. They make many attempts to estimate or guess at what is going on, but their preoccupation, quite naturally, is with that part of work and business which is counted, because they can measure, control, and tax that part. We must not, however, be deceived into thinking that it's only the formal, counted bit of the economy that matters. For instance, more than half of the whole population of this country are in the informal economy. Many of them are, of course, too young or too old to work in the market economy or the redistribution economy. Some of them are too busy running a home or bringing up children. A few of them, no doubt, find it more profitable because they work in the black economy part. Three million people, perhaps more, would not be there by choice and are registered for work in the two formal economies. All these people are in some way dependent on the redistribution economy (the state sector) for support in cash or kind. They use its roads, police, hospitals and schools even if they don't draw social benefit or pensions. All of them are customers of the market economy, even if they only buy their groceries from it. But none of them work in the market and redistribution economies. But they work, don't they? Ask any housewife, gardener, or young mother. It just does not get counted. And their work adds wealth, as we have seen, even if it never gets counted.

In Belgium it is against the law to paint your own house if you are unemployed. Crazy? Well, wait a minute. House painting is a profession, employing people. If everyone painted their own houses there would be no work for house-painters. If unemployed people

24

start painting their houses they will effectively be spreading their unemployment to others. Presumably if they do it in their spare time it is a leisure activity not 'job substitution'.

Work in the informal economy

Work in the informal economy often starts in the household, spreads to the voluntary economy and ends up in the commercial sector, hidden or open, as when the pâté made for home entertaining becomes demanded at local charity sales and ends up being made under contract for the local delicatessen. Other examples are:

Carpentry	Taxi service
Dressmaking	Photography
Tutoring	Typing
Book-keeping	Writing
Seedlings	Journalism
Job printing	Toy-making
Car maintenance	Pottery
Tree pruning	Plumbing
Vegetables	Housing consultancy
Horticultural advice	Painting
Computer programming	Translating
Interior decorating	Reading scripts
Indexing	Picture framing

A small brainstorming session could probably add another twenty.

It used to be cheaper to have other people to do the work you were less good at, such as plumbing or carpentry, whilst you spent your time and earned your money doing the things *you* were good at. That is no longer so true. It may make economic sense to take time off work to do your own maintenance and repair work. The saving in bills may be much more than you lose in wages. But the more we do things for ourself, the more we cut out jobs for others. Should we then outlaw DIY as job displacement or welcome it as self-sufficiency?

To the black economy and the household economy we must add the voluntary economy in which five million people do voluntary, unpaid, uncounted work every week in something like two hundred thousand different voluntary organisations. That is a lot of effort, adding work to our society in lots of different sectors of the community. If it all had to be paid for it would cost many millions. The informal economy, therefore, is made up of the black, the household, and the voluntary economies – all big, all growing and all outside our national accounting system.

It is important that we understand the differences between the market, the redistribution and the informal economies because it is the shifts from one to the other that are going to make all the difference

25

to the eighties, and particularly to those coming to the end of their working lives in the eighties. *There are five trends at work in the system:*

TREND NUMBER ONE

We are losing industries to the newly industrialised countries. One hundred and fifty years ago we discovered that other people could produce food more cheaply than we could. We started to import food (much to many people's horror) and used the labour which that released to make the manufactured goods which other nations needed. It was a structural shift in the economy. Today we have discovered that other nations can make many of those manufactured goods more cheaply than we can, mainly because they have much lower labour costs (up to ten times lower in some cases) and fewer restrictions on how they use that labour. First it was textiles and cameras that were cheaper, then ships and steel, now cars and televisions. We can hold up the process for a while by government subsidies to the disappearing industries, but the cost becomes prohibitive as we found with British Steel. We can hold on to bits of the 'special' market in each industry – fashion shoes, oil rigs instead of ships, sports cars and Range Rovers – but the overall trend is inevitable and against us. It is a *structural shift.*

What people earn in different countries
Average hourly pay in manufacturing industry in 1980: ·

	US $		US $
Belgium	13.18	Brazil	1.73
Netherlands	12.18	Mexico	2.76
Germany	11.94	Hong Kong	1.51
France	9.46	Singapore	1.09
Italy	9.01	South Korea	1.10
Britain	7.07	Taiwan	1.25

US Bureau of Labour Statistics

What then do we do with the labour which is released? Our competitive edge must be in our know-how, and our ability to turn that into an airbus, a bio-chemical plant or an international banking service. These know-how industries and services have to be the growth areas of the future *but:*
1 We are in competition with the other industrial countries which face the same trends as ourselves

2 You need an awful lot of them to make up for all the jobs lost in British Steel, and the other older industries
3 The jobs require skills and training radically different from those possessed by the average industrial worker or manager, skills, moreover, which are hard to acquire unless you started doing so in your schooldays.

TREND NUMBER TWO

Machines are replacing people. We have been substituting capital equipment for labour steadily over the last ten years and the new micro-technologies based on the silicon chip will allow us to go on doing that for a long time to come. Sometimes the reductions are dramatic; one factory, for example, installed new computer-controlled mixing and blending equipment and reduced the workers in that department from thirty-four to six in one go. Great for productivity, lousy for jobs. Sometimes, however, the labour substitution is much smaller. Eight thousand industrial robots in Japan are calculated to have replaced only sixteen thousand jobs, making their main contribution in accuracy and precision. Technology is not always a demon. Indeed, when the work which the machines take over is dangerous, dirty, or monotonous there is little resistance. Paint-shops in automobile plants have never been the most popular work-places and automation is to be welcomed.

It is when the machines take over more of the supervisory and co-ordinating work that many more will complain. Office work is always singled out as the most likely one for major shifts from people to machines because the new technology is so adept at information processing. It is, of course, true that new technologies always create new jobs. Video-recorders, for instance, need to be manufactured and tapes created for them to play. The evidence so far, however, is that the new industries are not going to need as much labour as the ones they displace. Output they can provide, and wealth for themselves and the nation if they are well run, but not that many jobs. We should not delude ourselves.

If we cannot create new markets for new goods and services – the structural shift – we will be in a state of what has been called absolute as opposed to relative automation. That means that labour is not released for new and growing industries, it is just released, period. The big question for all the industrialised countries is therefore whether they can find enough saleable services and high-technology industries to make up for the ones we are all losing. Britain hits the problem first because her industries were the oldest and therefore the first to go. First in, first out.

27

The changing technology

Anyone who wants a reliable guide to what technology will be doing to us and for us should have a look at Japan's thirty-year industrial plan, drawn up by the Agency for Industrial Science and Technology. Since Japan has a habit of turning plans into self-fulfilling prophecies, this is more than mere crystal-ball gazing. It will probably happen.

Within the next five years, Japanese manufacturers are expected to produce car engines made entirely from ceramics, light and resistant to heat. Chemical plants will turn out large quantities of artificial blood. At the same time Japan will see more sophisticated robots and more unmanned factories, building up to a new generation of computerised robots which take their own decisions and understand ordinary conversation. By the end of the century they are expected to be able to touch, see and taste as well as hear and talk. Word processors, by then, will be translating foreign business letters into Japanese.

Japan's trains will have no wheels or moving parts but will glide around silently on a magnetic cushion at speeds up to 325 m.p.h. Within twenty years artificial limbs will be so sophisticated that the handicapped will be able to participate in most forms of sport, while the blind will have artificial eyes. We will be wearing television sets on our wrists and carrying telephones in our pockets. Medical advances will provide the average Japanese of the next century with a life-span of one hundred years.

TREND NUMBER THREE

As a consequence of the first two trends the numbers of jobs in the market economy are shrinking. In the last ten years nearly two million jobs were lost in productive industry.

Some were picked up by growing service industries but in total nearly one million jobs moved out of the market economy. This was essential in order to remain competitive at home and abroad, because to remain competitive our efficiency has to keep pace with our rivals and improve by at least two-and-a-half per cent per year. Recently it has been doing even better than that, by as much as six per cent in manufacturing industry in 1981. But what that really means is that we have been using fewer people to produce much the same output. To improve efficiency *and* increase jobs you have to grow much faster than two-and-a-half per cent per year. Japan has been able to do that. Britain has not been able to do so because she has not yet been able to manage that structural shift. We shall be doing well if we can achieve two-and-half per cent per annum in order to hold the total number of jobs steady in the market economy. But there will be one million extra people (over and above those retiring) entering the labour market from school in the next decade. The market economy is not likely to provide any of those extra wanted jobs.

TREND NUMBER FOUR

In the 1970s all those one million jobs discarded by the market economy were picked up in the redistribution economy – the state employed them in one way or another. In 1980, there were actually more people in employment than ever before in this country. Unfortunately, there were at that time still another two million who wanted jobs and didn't get them. But the number of jobs in the state sector has now stopped growing. This is partly because the government has refused to borrow more money. Even if future governments do spend more money, it is likely to go mostly into capital projects which will give much-needed work to the market economy (and stop more jobs leaving that economy). Since there will be an extra one million people net coming onto the labour market in the eighties, there is bound to be a slow continuing increase in unemployment, unless, that is, we find another way of occupying them. What happens to all those who cannot find work in the market economy or the redistribution economy? They go into the informal economy where they are supported by money from the redistribution economy. This will be so although, ironically, it now costs almost the same amount to maintain someone unemployed in the informal economy as it would to employ him in a government office.

TREND NUMBER FIVE

There will therefore be more and more people living and 'working' in the informal economy. They will not all be on the fiddle in the black economy. A lot of them will be working at home, doing things for themselves and their neighbours. They will be working in the many different voluntary organisations around the country. They will be watching and participating in sport. They will not be spending as much money, because they won't have as much, but by doing things for themselves, spending less on travel to work, clothes for work, meals at work, they may retain their quality of life on a lower expenditure. Yet, because it happens to be at home, in the household economy, all their work and output does not get counted, nor taxed – it is, in a sense, drained away from the business world, the market economy. If you make your own clothes, you are draining work away from business, just as you are if you grow your own potatoes instead of buying them, or ride a bicycle instead of driving the car and buying petrol.

Because there are going to be more people in this informal economy, with time and skills and energy to spare, but little money, we are going to see more of what has been called the self-service society. After all, the average home now has as many machines in it as a small textile factory had at the turn of the century. With our drills and our sewing machines, our cookers and radios, we can be very self-sufficient as long as the electricity is working.

IS IT INEVITABLE?

If you look around you can see these trends at work all over the country. Everyone will have watched the unemployment figures grow in Britain and in all the European countries. It looks, and is, traumatic to many.

Do we have to lose so many jobs to the informal economy? Many hope not, but they pin their hopes onto different strategies.

One strategy looks for a revival of the market economy at home and abroad and regards the recent slimming down of the work force as a necessary preliminary to more vigorous competitive action. One part of that action would be an attempt to recover bits of our own home market which we have lost to competition in Europe and America who ought not to be able to make things more cheaply than we can. Another part of it requires us to make that structural shift into new technologies and new saleable services in order to keep ahead of everyone else. It is a strategy calling for constantly improving productivity and more and more investment. The trouble with improving productivity is that it shakes out old jobs as fast or faster than it creates new ones. A recent look at the consequences of the most optimistic forecasts of capital expenditure in industry concluded that they would result in a net *loss* of six hundred thousand jobs.

It is essential that this strategy is given all the impetus possible, because we need the new wealth, both abroad and at home, which it can create, but if it can even hold the jobs in the market economy to their present level we shall be doing better than we have done in the past fifteen years.

A second strategy puts more responsibility on government, wanting more capital investment in the infrastructure of society and more direct employment in the redistribution economy, and forget about any restrictions on borrowing for the future. Capital projects would undoubtedly create more jobs in the market economy as builders, railway engineers and many others moved to meet the new orders. Similarly a looser rein on public expenditure would at least prevent the run-down of teachers and local government staff. It is true that interest rates and perhaps wage rates and therefore inflation would tend to rise as a result of any relaxation but jobs at least would be created. However, even the most ambitious estimates do not claim to create more than one million new jobs. This would not happen all at once but it would at least pick up the extra slack caused by the one million new workers arriving over the next ten years.

A *third strategy* believes that work has a higher priority than full freedom of choice and would move us towards what is called a 'command economy' where wages are controlled, imports regulated and labour directed. That way you could revive the domestic market, concentrate resources on the structural shift and push labour into areas where work was needed even if no-one was particularly inclined to go there. The French approach of indicative planning and state ownership of key industries is perhaps one step towards this strategy. It has a logic behind it in its argument that the market, left to itself, is too short-term in its thinking and too anxious about profit. But the French still find that their unemployment is growing.

A *fourth view*, a little more fatalistically, looks ahead to the end of that influx, in the mid-1990s, when the potential labour force may actually be dropping as more people retire than join, and argues that we just need to sit it out.

Linked to this view is the theory of long-wave economic cycles, originally proposed by Kondratiev, a Russian economist. This theory holds that the world's economic booms come in forty-five year cycles, each new wave being preceded by the dislocations of major technological change. We are in the trough of a wave right now, experiencing all the dislocation, but the crest is due at the end of the century when our workforce will be in better shape. But will it also be better equipped to take advantage of the new boom?

There are good arguments for all four strategies, although the last one is too passive to be acceptable to most people. I myself would prefer a judicious blend of the first three strategies for they are not incompatible. But this book is not a treatise on economic policy. It is only my concern to alert people in their fifties to the likely future. The truth has to be that whatever strategy or blend of strategies we pursue over the next decade we cannot provide all the people who want jobs with the full-time life-time jobs which they want at the pay levels they desire. Something has to give. It is unlikely to be pay for we are still badly paid by comparison with our neighbours. All the indications are that it will be a combination of the other two factors and that there will be fewer, shorter jobs. What this means in practice will be discussed in the next chapter.

We must however be careful to distinguish between output and employment. We can increase our wealth and prosperity as a nation without increasing the number of people who work. Indeed, in the market economy, that is the only way we can do it. The structural shift in our economic activity means, therefore, a gradual structural shift of people and work into the informal economy, so that we have a *dual economy*, formal and informal.

Disappearing jobs

	1966	*1972*	*1979*
Number of people employed in productive industries in Britain	11,852,000	9,814,000	9,010,000
Index of output in productive industries to Britain	90.6	102.3	113.5

Cotton:	In 1914 there were 710,000 workers In 1979 there were 66,800

Wool:	In 1911 there were 261,000 workers In 1979 there were 73,000

The new Carrington Viyella Mill at Atherton in Lancashire cost six million pounds but needs only 95 workers.

Because we got there first

Percentage of all workers who were employed in industry in 1961		Increase or decrease in industrial work-force 1961–1975
UK	48.8%	−15.8%
West Germany	49.6%	−11.6%
Italy	38.2%	+ 7.9%
France	31.1%	+11.1%
USA	32.8%	−12.2%
Japan	29.9%	+27.5%

Traumatic though the scenario is to many who feel they are its victims there are many positive side-effects. Some individuals are pushed into a new pattern of life which, after the initial shock, can be stimulating and fun. Businesses find that after the pain of a redundancy programme they do much better with a slimmed down staff. There is the beginning of a drift away from big cities to country towns. But huge questions loom up.

QUESTION NUMBER ONE

Who is going to pay for it all?

All those in the redistribution economy or in the informal economy have to have something to live on. It may be a wage, a salary, a pension or some form of benefit, but it all has to come out of taxation. So do the resources, and equipment, the roads, the machinery, even the buildings which are used in the redistribution economy. A large proportion of that tax comes from the incomes of those who work. Another, slightly larger, chunk comes from levies (VAT or duty) on what they buy. If fewer people are working and more are being supported the gap between the government's income and expenditure must increase. If people are buying less and making more themselves, the tax from goods and services will not do much to help.

Britain's money

Did you know that:

1 In 1978/9, Britain's total public expenditure was over £65 billion? Of which
£15 billion went on Social Security
£9 billion went on Education
£8 billion went on Health and Social Services, and
£7 billion went on Defence

2 In 1978 taxes on income produced £22 billion
Taxes on expenditure produced £23 billion

3 The Public Sector employs 1 in every 3 of all Britain's workers

4 1 in 20 of all people in the UK received supplementary benefits in 1980

5 14 countries spend MORE on health per individual than Britain does

6 countries spend MORE on Social Security per individual than Britain does

From *Know Your Society*

It would be tempting for a government to raise the rate of income tax. As the Prime Minister of Southern Ireland said when defending his proposed tax increases in 1982 'It is only right that those at work should pay more for those out of work'. But this could lead to a self-defeating spiral. If taxes rise, wages will rise to compensate, leading to more pressures in firms to shed labour to keep down costs. This means that there are even fewer people paying taxes tempting government to raise the tax yet again to keep their total revenue up. And so on, and so on. But not only might big increases in income tax be self-defeating, they could lead to great divides in society. Those who pay tax would increasingly resent the growing burdens they have to bear. Those who receive it will still resent what they see as the large salaries of those who pay the tax. Both parties will feel injured and hard done by.

An alternative is to increase the taxes on what we spend, not what we earn. Governments may find it simpler to raise the taxes and charges on products – including charges for services in the redistribution economy. The problem is then to stop this kicking-off a rise in the cost of living as the effective price of everything goes up. It is a fairer method of taxation in one sense in that everyone pays it, or can choose not to pay it by not buying things.

On the other hand, taxes on goods and services bear proportionately more heavily on the poor than on the rich, because there are some things which everyone has to buy, like them or not.

There are no easy answers to the questions. Committees of one sort and another have been investigating them for years. One of the most interesting was the Meade Committee which suggested that the whole basis of taxation should be changed to concentrate on taxing what we spend rather than what we earn. They did not mean increasing the taxes on goods and services, but rather that people should declare their expenditure rather than their income (thus, amongst other things, encouraging people to save, not spend). This would seem to be a fairer way of taxing people and fairness is going to have to be a crucial element in taxation policy in the eighties. More money will have to be found somehow, but it must be seen to come from all and not from a few if we are to avoid an increasingly resentful society.

QUESTION NUMBER TWO

How can Britain get richer?
A richer economy will not, I have argued, necessarily bring more jobs but it will greatly ease the burdens of those in and out of jobs. Unfortunately we are the prisoners of our history. The peak of Britain's industrial and economic greatness was 1870, over a hundred years ago. Ever since then, other countries have been catching up and eventually overtaking us in economic prosperity. The trouble with leading in the first lap of the long-distance race is that you wear yourself out, and this is effectively what happened to Britain. We were the first to turn an agricultural population into an effective industrial workforce, the first to export on a large scale, the first to understand about investing in capital equipment and new technology. But that was in the nineteenth century. In 1940, we were technically bankrupt after the first year of the war, and had, effectively, to be bailed out by our American friends, so far had we fallen down the economic slopes. Can we discover the powers of invention, the taste for risk and the energy for promotion which characterised the early Victorians? Many suspect that we cannot – that the country's talents have long been turned towards the professions, the arts, and government. Our police are still

world-renowned, our theatre and television the envy of all, our lawyers, teachers, doctors, accountants, and financial experts known to be excellent. In the eyes of the world, Britain is a country where it is marvellous to live, terrible to do business in. Unfortunately, a society which concentrates on the professions, theatre, and services does not find it easy to earn the foreign currency it needs to pay for its foreign purchases. Tourists may flock to our theatres and hotels and stores, but they do not easily compensate for a lost export contract for jet engines, nuclear power plants, or a batch of ships. Without a manufacturing base which makes things which other people need and will pay for, or services like banking or design which are saleable overseas, we shall revert to a 'declined society' with great limitations on our choices and way of life.

Industries, like everything else, have lives. They grow, mature and then decline. We have become so experienced in the management of declining industries, that we have forgotten the ways of growing industries. We have to invest in the unknown – temperamentally difficult for cautious bankers. We have to grow a huge base of potential industrial talent in our schools and colleges and universities – difficult when money is so tight. We have to make it fashionable and rewarding to be a technological explorer once again. That is the nature of the structural shift which is required in our economy.

It is only by the most imaginative combination of brains and new machinery that Britain will be able to make anything that the outside world requires. There will, of course, be lots of scope to make things for ourselves which other people now make. It is, for instance, crazy economics that the wire trolleys in my East Anglian supermarket should all be made in West Germany. Here again, however, they won't be made competitively by using old-fashioned methods with lots of expensive workers, but by automated machinery, well made and well maintained. Not many jobs perhaps, but lots of wire trolleys.

There are signs, small signs, that those needs are now recognised. It is hard to believe that we shall see any results in less than a generation, for these are long-term conditions that have to be changed. In the short term, we might encourage foreign talent, the Americans, Japanese and Asians – to use Britain as their manufacturing plot. We are greatly helped in the medium term by the North Sea oil production, but it has drained off a huge amount of investment and technological talent into an industry which may well have quite a short life.

One thing seems to be clear. The new generation of manufacturing industries will not need a lot of unskilled workers. The new industries will be full of very expensive equipment, needling highly skilled people to design, build, and maintain it. The workforce in such industries will mainly be specialist with a small semi-skilled group who will

35

really be feeding the machines. Capital equipment will have replaced labour in manufacturing just as it has done in the fields and sheds of Britain's farms. Likewise, the new saleable services will be specialist, high-skill, and backed by sophisticated equipment. They will provide jobs for the young, the intelligent, and the well-educated.

QUESTION NUMBER THREE

Who will get the jobs?
Traditionally, a job has meant the three forty-eights (forty-eight hours a week, forty-eight weeks a year, for forty-eight years). It seems a lot, but even in 1980 the average unskilled worker was working for-ty-six hours (including overtime) with perhaps five and a half weeks holiday (including public holidays), and was retiring in his early six-ties having started at fourteen or fifteen. That comes out at 3 × 46. Only two per cent of British male workers work part-time although the figure is forty per cent for women.

There are not going to be enough 3 × 46 jobs for all who want them.

How should we apportion the jobs that do exist (and there will still be twenty-four million of them)?

At present the system works on the 'finders keepers' principle. If you are clever or lucky enough to have a job you hold on to it as long as possible. This inevitably means that those who are less skilled, less experienced, less capable, or less lucky, get left out – pushed into un-employment, or, in my terms, pushed into the informal economy. It is young people, particularly those with no qualifications, no CSE results, it is immigrants, the handicapped, and women who lose out in the scramble for jobs. Yet those people are precisely those who will find it most difficult to survive on their own in the informal economy. Instead of the informal economy being a place of freedom, choice and self-sufficiency, it is in danger of becoming the scrap-heap of society.

Will priorities change? There are signs that they may. Training jobs for young people are now firmly embedded in the policy of all parties. They disagree only about the precise terms and conditions. Early retirement options are becoming much more widespread, and more readily taken up. The older worker is beginning to give place to youth, but disadvantaged minorities are still disadvantaged in this particular competition for work. If society has to choose and all the signs are that it must, then fairness suggests that if anyone has to move into the informal economy it ought to be the older worker who should have a reservoir of skills and experience, and perhaps even of money, to help him or her survive. Will the older worker see it that way? Will we see it that way?

WHAT DOES ALL THIS MEAN FOR THE FIFTIES

There will be less full-time work for them and less money. Those conclusions seem inescapable. There will be pockets of growth in the formal economy – in personal services and in new technology – but they will be of little help to most people who are in their fifties.

It is understandable if fifty-year-olds feel cheated. After thirty-odd years of work to have the rules changed on you in the last part of the game is tough indeed. 'What', many asked themselves, 'have we done to deserve this?' 'I have worked steadily and well for thirty-five years,' one steel worker said, 'How do they have the right to stop it all without even asking me?' 'They' would much rather it had not to happen. We are in the grip of forces beyond the control of governments – forces like the birth of new ideas and the maturing of new nations. Britain is not insulated from the world or from nature.

All, however, is not bleak. The new game contains many possibilities as the next chapter makes clear. But it does require a determination to play the new game and not the old. I have argued in this chapter that there is a structural shift, requiring new thinking, for the old ways will not work so well any more. It is time to consider what will work, how technological change can be a social dividend for *all* society, how a new social consensus can be established which apportions that dividend fairly, and how new definitions of success and happiness in life can emerge.

Edmund Burke, in cynical mood, once wrote 'To complain of the age we live in, to murmur at the present possessors of power, to lament the past, to conceive extravagant hopes of the future, are the common dispositions of the greater part of mankind.'

The sample of the people of Britain who talked to me before I wrote this book were more realistic than Edmund Burke would have believed, as the following quotations illustrate.

The fifties look at the eighties

'Bleak, very bleak for the next ten years. There will be a struggle, like in the jungle, and then there must, there just must be some light at the end of the tunnel.'
Toolmaker in Doncaster

'There will be a lot more out of work . . . the only way I can see it getting back to full employment, and I should hate it to happen, is war.'
Teacher in Cumbernauld

'We as a society have become materialistic. Kids today expect £30 or £40 spent on them as a present, whereas when we were kids sixpence was a lot of money, and they don't know how to occupy their time. The kids are bought things to make them happy or to shut them up. And

---

Cont.

37

they are not educated for its own sake but for A-levels or whatever, and they are not going to have the jobs that go on until they are 65, because we've not got them now. So what's going to happen? If we've got more leisure time, what are we going to do with it?'
Housewife in Romford

'Over the last few years it's been a consumer society . . . there's got to be a re-think about that sort of society. In my opinion the peak is going to be reached in what you can manufacture, consume, dispose of, and I can't see that it's going to go back to full employment for five to ten years. This will mean that there's got to be some different type of society afterwards.'
Retired man in Wolverhampton

CHAPTER THREE

WORK OR WHAT?

'I think at our age there's still a lot of work left in us and we want to be used. We're the wrong age to be put on the scrap heap.'

'If you don't have something to work at, you'll end up a cabbage.'

'I don't like standing in my window seeing my wife go to work.'

One group of fifty-year-old men, asked how they saw the next ten years, talked only about *work*, or the lack of it. They were all men, it is true, for men in our society have been accustomed to a job for the whole of their active life. The three forty-eights was their entitlement. It has even been included in the Universal Declaration of Human Rights, 'everyone has the right to work, to have free choice of employment, to just and favourable conditions of work and to protection against unemployment'. The United Nations made that declaration, thirty-four years ago, when these ideals seemed both reasonable and attainable. No wonder that many feel cheated. Society has promised what it cannot deliver. Is that the fault of the fifty-five-year-old redundant buying clerk, or the seventeen-year-old unwanted youth on Merseyside. No, clearly it is not their fault, but it is their problem, a problem which is not going to go away for the foreseeable future.

But work in the form of jobs is not only disappearing, it is changing; whether we grow fast or grow slow or grow not at all. This is mainly because of new technical possibilities, but partly because of some changes in society's values. We need first to look at some of these changes and then to consider how they will affect people in their fifties. 'Work', however, is a bigger word than 'job'. It may not be counted by economists or statisticians but work goes on in the home, in the community, and in the garden, in the informal economy, as I have described. We will need to consider what the other kinds of work may be and what the options are for those in their fifties. And, finally, there is the other side of work – leisure. What does leisure really mean? Can we have too much of it or too little? How does one get a proper balance? Why do we need work at all?

PATTERNS OF WORK

A job, as I outlined in the last chapter, used to mean the three forty-eights of 48 hours by 48 weeks by 48 years. The three forty-eights are breaking down. It is not only that people want shorter working weeks and longer holidays. There are signs that the whole way in which work is organised, and people paid to do it, is beginning to be modified at the edges. It may be that the changes haven't happened yet where you are. It does depend on what business or activity you find yourself in, for the changes affect some types of work more quickly than others, but the changes *are* happening, and, whatever happens to the economy, they will be affecting more and more lives as the 1980s move on. Changes usually start at the edges and creep towards the centre of things. Look to the edges if you want a clue to the future for it is at those edges that you will see some of the following changes.

FEES NOT WAGES

If you pay a person a wage, you buy his or her *time*, which you can then, within reason, use for your purposes. If you pay someone or some people a fee you buy their *work*, whether it be a product or a service.

Self-employed individuals charge fees. They may be professionals, such as lawyers and accountants or architects, or they may be craftsmen. Organisations charge fees to their customers but pay the people who work for them wages, because they have bought their time. Naturally, you include the cost of your time when calculating your fee but you are, in the end, selling the fruits of your labour, not your labour.

Traditionally in Britain, organisations have liked to buy people's time and then put it to work for them. A larger proportion of the working population (ninety-two per cent) work for a wage here than in any other country. We seem to prefer to sell our time rather than our work. We may lose a bit of freedom thereby but we win some security. But that security is now part of the problem, for organisations are beginning to find that the wage contract does not in fact give them the freedom they expected. It used to be sensible for a firm to keep control of all the operations which affected its business, by employing everyone they needed. It suited the firms and it suited the employees. Firms did, and still do, *employ* people to run their own printing operations, their own small travel agencies to make travel arrangements for their executives, they *employ* cooks and waiters, chauffeurs and accountants. That way, they have everything under their own organisational roof. But today if you pay a wage you also pay a lot of costs on top of that. There is national insurance, effectively a payroll tax, which is burden enough on the employer, but in addition the employer has to heat, light, and often feed his employees while they work for him. In the case of office workers he has in effect to give them a day-time home. The additional overhead cost of employing somebody usually at least equals the original cost of the wage. More than that – if he employs somebody today he has them for life; it is like adopting a child. For the employee the wage means security, perhaps. For the employer it is beginning to seem more of a burden than a convenience.

Home in the office

A foreign visitor to the management floor of a large corporation was struck by the new fashion in office furnishings amongst the managers. Each office was furnished like a sitting-room. Desks were out. Sofas and low tables, book cases and artistic paintings were in. There was even a bar discreetly concealed in the more important offices. A delightful secretary brought coffee. A well-dressed young man, an assistant, briefed his manager on the day's events and arranged cars and chauffeurs.

'I see,' said the visitor, 'that the English have recreated the English country house in their executive offices. There is the small drawing-room, the maid, the butler and the chauffeur. How clever!

Office in the home

Joan Wilkins runs a UK homeworkers' agency employing some two thousand people on an irregular basis. Straight copy-typing and low-level clerical work make up a significant part of Wilkins's caseload, but higher skilled work predominates. The agency includes market researchers, town planners, graphic designers, proof-readers, indexers, economic researchers, translators and conference organisers.

Reported by David Clutterbuck and Roy Hill in *The Re-making of Work*

Organisations are therefore re-thinking the advantages of the wage contract. If they hired out, or sub-contracted, various bits of their work they would lose some control, perhaps, but they would also be able to slim down their overheads and reduce their commitments to so many people. The sub-contracting may be done with individuals, or with groups. Do the transport companies need to *employ* (for a wage) all their lorry drivers? No, and many lorry drivers are independent contractors working for a fee on a contract. Do small firms need to employ (for a wage) someone to do their accounts? No, but they do need to have their accounts done (for a fee). It is, for many organisations, a different way of working, requiring different management skills, but it should not be all that strange, for it already happens all around us. Builders (small and large) have always worked this way. The boards outside any major construction work effectively describe a temporary alliance of sub-contractors, all working for a negotiated fee. On a large site these sub-contractors will be firms who will themselves employ some people for a wage, but some will then be sub-contractors themselves. The stage, the film world, journals and newspapers, orchestras – the arts have long been familiar with the fee principle, for these are less predictable businesses than most and need the flexibility of the fee contract. Solicitors, accountants, and other professionals, have always worked for fees. Agriculture, too, has reduced the number of employees to the bare minimum and will sub-contract some of the occasional seasonal operations to outside specialists.

The ways of the builders and stage impresarios are gradually being adopted by other organisations. It makes economic sense for the business in unpredictable times, because the individual bears the burden of the uncertainty, not the organisation. Like it or not, and most of us won't, the fee will become as common as the wage. We shall look at the implications for the fifties generation shortly.

Sub-contracting as a way of life

One firm in West Germany has pushed sub-contracting as far as it will go with an extended system of sub-contracting, or franchising as it is sometimes called.

The firm manufacturers, sells and services a range of electrical motors throughout West Germany. They licence a number of small firms to make the motors to their design and agree to pay a fixed price for each motor as long as it passes their strict quality control procedures. They then license a number of agents to sell their motors in different areas of the country, agreeing to sell the motors to them at a certain price and to provide some advertising (designed by an advertising agency). The maintenance and service contracts are let out to other independents. Each licence runs for five years and may, or may not, be renewed. The firm employs (for a wage) a group of expert designers and some quality inspectors, but only needs one accountant and no personnel staff. They have, therefore, a tiny head office and are very profitable. In Britain, Marks and Spencers license manufacturers. The motor companies license selling and repair agents. The new Channel 4 on television plans to sub-contract the making of programmes but to keep overall control. Could local government do the same? Could schools?

TOOLS NOT MACHINES

Schumacher (the author of *Small is Beautiful*) once described a tool as something which was the servant of man, whereas man was the servant of a machine. At the time of the industrial revolution man's tools, in the villages and the fields, were clearly inefficient compared with the big machines driven by water and steam which were being developed. Men and women were forced, economically, to discard their tools and went to work at the machines. Note: they went *to* the machines. The machines had to be near the sources of power (water or coal) or the raw materials (iron, steel or clay), so the work and the people went to where the machines were, in the factories. Later, the machines became assembly lines powered by oil and then electricity, needing huge sheds to house them and continuous operation to be effective. Work continued to go to where the machines were.

The silicon chip is beginning to change all that and this is one of its main effects. It may or may not destroy lots of jobs; we don't know for sure. But it will certainly change the way work is done because of the whole micro-technology which it makes possible. Because of the tiny size of the chip, its reliability and its cheapness, it is turning the *machines* into *tools*. They are very sophisticated tools, it is true, and often quite big. We call them robots, automated production functions or numerically controlled machines, but they are really very special tools because they can be controlled by one or two persons – they are servants again, demanding and expensive servants, but servants none the less. The effect will be to move the work and the tools to where the people are, rather than the other way round, subtly reversing the movement of the industrial revolution.

Not much has happened yet but you can already see some changes inside factories. Individual work-stations, or the 'job-shop' are becoming more common, where an individual or small group can complete a whole sequence of operations on their own. They can put together a complete radio, weld a whole car, make a chair, not just bits of one. It will go farther. Some tools – not the robot welders of the car factories perhaps – are small enough to be carried, but capable of doing very complex and sophisticated tasks. Why should they remain, all of them, in the same shed? Why can't they go to the homes of the workers, or at least to work-places nearer their homes? After all, the energy for these new tools is electricity and electricity can be installed anywhere. Only the raw material presents a problem, and the transport of the finished goods. Maybe more work will take place nearer to where the customer is than to where the raw material is, since it will usually be more expensive to transport the final, packaged, product than the raw materials.

The substitution of tools for machines means the end of giant 'works', communities in themselves supporting communities around them. Towns like Corby and Consett, dominated by the industrial architecture of one organisation, will never happen again. Maybe that is for the best but those huge work communities did provide many jobs, including jobs which were often not directly related to the task of producing steel. The new work communities will be smaller. They won't have the number of layers of command in them, nor the battalions of supporting staff to which we are used. Even canteens may become a rare sight, unless organisations club together to support a common eating-place.

Small plants and offices do not, however, necessarily mean more small businesses. Those small plants will, more often than not, be owned by big businesses, for in that way the economies of scale can be preserved, with standard designs, marketing and costing. Bigness and smallness will have to learn to live together in a new sort of organisational federation.

Small plants and offices (probably with less than four hundred people each) are more friendly, pleasanter places, but there are drawbacks, for life never sends blessings without their accompanying problems. A small plant does not offer the same scope for life-time careers. There is just not room to keep on *everybody* who joins at sixteen until they are sixty-four (the forty-eight years), because the business would not then be able to bring in any new talent or skills. Small plants rely on people leaving to keep the momentum going and they rely on those that stay being prepared to learn new skills and new trades. Things cannot stand still in small plants. If they do, they get abandoned by the big businesses which own them, for it is always easier to close or sell a small plant than a big one. Flexibility, change, and learning are, or will be, key words for the small organisations of tomorrow. They may be more fun, these organisations, but they cannot be so secure or predictable as the ones we grew up in, even though they will, most of them, be under the umbrella of a big federal organisation.

Small is necessary

'People don't *obey* any more, they agree, if you're lucky.' The speaker was a manager, speaking ruefully of the difficulties of running an organisation in a free democracy.

'You cannot *tell* us what to do, you can only *ask* us and if it's sensible we will of course agree.' The speaker was a shop steward explaining to a young manager the reality of life.

A meeting of managers of successful companies was trying to find some common causes for their success. They discovered that in one respect they had a common philosophy; all plants and offices should be small enough to be run with only two levels of supervision between the man at the top and the man at the bottom because only then could one be sure that the manager could know everyone on the site, and only if he knew them and they knew him could you have management by

Cont.

agreement. 'How can you agree with someone you don't know? Anonymity requires obedience, which is only given reluctantly.'

This principle put an effective ceiling on the size of individual operations – probably around three hundred people. Small may not be beautiful but it is becoming necessary if people are to be treated the way they want to be treated.

One way in which the 'Small is Necessary' trend makes itself felt is in the current crop of management *buy-outs*. In a buy-out a group of managers and workers buy out their plant or operation from the parent company which would otherwise have closed it down because it was not paying its way. Finance is partly provided by the men themselves but mainly by a friendly financing source such as a bank or, in Britain, the Industrial and Commercial Finance Corporation (ICFC) which specialises in financing small businesses. Five years ago the phenomenon was virtually unknown but in 1982 ICFC alone expects to be involved in a hundred such operations. Panache Upholstery of Leeds was the most publicised of the buy-outs in 1980, but the biggest yet is the £53,000,000 deal by which the employees of the National Freight Corporation are buying their company from the Government. Panache emerged from the collapse of A & M Upholstery. Bob Wilkins, its managing director, convinced sixty employees to put in all their redundancy money and raised enough outside loans to save the venture. Small has so far turned out to be profitable, particularly when backed with your own money.

TERMINALS NOT TRAINS

The other effect of the chip technology is more noticeable – it is the growth of terminals, or the Visual Display Units which sit on the top of small computers, or are attached to them by telephone wires. A television set in an office these days is not there for the cricket commentaries but as part of the communications system built around the computer. You don't have to talk to someone nowadays to give them information or to ask questions, you talk to their terminal, or rather your terminal talks to theirs. Small groups cannot work like that, of course, with such a remote-controlled artificial way of communicating, but different parts of an organisation can. One department talks to another by paper (memos) or the telephone. It then costs less if the departments are in the same building. But get them talking through the computer and it does not really matter whether they are in the same building or even in the same country. One British organisation, doing some sophisticated design work, found the cheapest way for one department to talk to another was to use a computer in Los Angeles in the middle of their night but our day, when the charges were very low, bouncing their signals off a satellite. We don't need to be that extreme but we must start to question whether it is necessary to bring everyone in to large offices in big cities, where space is very expensive, when we are going to talk to them through the computer anyway. Why not put them into much cheaper offices in the suburbs or small towns, so that the organisation saves on rents and rates and the individual saves his or her rail fares and all the wear and tear of commuting?

Individuals and organisations in different countries were asked, in a recent survey, about their preferences and plans for part-time working and home working.

Part time work

Do you expect the proportion of part-timers in your organisation to increase in the next five years?

	% answering 'yes'
Average of 10 European Countries	40.3
Netherlands (Highest)	54.7
Spain (Lowest)	12.9
UK	20.8

Working from Home

Do you see the possibility of more people working from home in the next decade?

	% answering 'yes'
Average of 10 European Countries	22.4
Netherlands (Highest)	34.9
Germany (Lowest)	7.8
UK	16.8

Working from home

If you, individually, could work from home all or part of the week, would you prefer to do so?

	% answering 'yes'
Average of 10 European Countries	35.5
Netherlands (Highest)	50.0
Sweden (Lowest)	18.9
UK	40.8

Note the big difference between what individuals in the UK would like and the intentions of organisations. Which will prevail?

From D. Clutterbuck and R. Hill, *The Re-Making of Work*

Control Data in the USA is running a pilot project with a group of 'telecommuters' in which each individual has two work-places, his home or a desk in a satellite office close to his home as well as a shared desk in one of the company's main offices. People in France are talking of four hundred thousand people working at remote terminals by 1990. That may be over-ambitious but the USA estimates that a hundred thousand people are already subscribing to time-sharing information services via home terminals in that country. A lot depends on the availability and accessibility of the equipment, particularly of the telephone lines to carry the traffic, but by 1990 the UK hopes to have optical fibre cables dealing with a quarter of all trunk calls. The technology is ready-made for home-based computer programmers and firms like F. International with six hundred employees, all home-based, in the UK take full advantage of it already. But more and more companies are expanding their numbers of remote-controlled sales people, researchers, and analysts.

Does homework equal poverty?

The textile industry has a long tradition of exploiting homeworkers. Andrea Waind, in New Society of 1 March 1982, has compiled a list of horror stories.

Jan Smith was paid 24 pence per *day* for making up handbags. Now she stitches linings to girl's shoe uppers, a process called post-machining. 'Dead boring', she says, but at least it's better paid and the conditions are better than her last job – insole binding. 'You stick the soles on with awful glues – you can see the fumes coming off. The house is full of boards with big men's boots drying and the smell of the glue.' The average pay for this sort of homework was £50 to £60 a week in 1981, but there is usually no contract, and there is no holiday pay and no sick pay.

Rogue employers, health hazards and tedium are typical, says Andrea Waind. The Leicester Outwork Campaign has been set up to give women working at home more information and advice and to bring employers and unions together to discuss possible action. They produce a Fact Pack which is in great demand nationally. Most enquiries, they say, are about national insurance and income tax because homeworkers' legal status is doubtful, they can be self-employed under tax law and employed under labour law.

There are estimated to be between one and four hundred thousand homeworkers in Britain today. Councils are supposed to keep registers of homeworkers but they only know if employers tell them. Not all do. If homeworking is to increase, society must make sure that the exploitation of the textile workers is not repeated in the new technologies.

More and more organisations are beginning to make the calculation and discovering that whole departments can be moved out of the centre without any loss of efficiency. The commuter may, eventually, be a dying breed and British Rail may find that its trains are travelling the wrong way. It will take years, of course, if not decades to switch the whole scene, but the signs are already there at the edges.

WHAT DOES IT ALL ADD UP TO?

Britain used to have the largest proportion of large organisations, both in business and government, of any European country. She still has, but those organisations are changing their shape. They are getting spread out, into smaller more distant bits, and those bits are increasingly contracting out some of their work to smaller groups or to individuals. The management of shrinking organisations is suddenly a fashionable topic.

Life is going to be less secure and less comfortable for anyone who has thought of themselves as working for an organisation, being the organisation's property, but also its responsibility, to use as it saw fit but also to support, reward, and develop, unless and until he or she chose to resign or was criminally negligent. Those sorts of 'organisation careers' are going to become very limited, certainly in business. They will continue longer in government and local government because there is more predictability there and less pressure from technology or competition.

On the other hand, if you see yourself as a person with a skill or a talent to sell, who enjoys independence and is prepared to trade a little security for more freedom, then the world that is coming will suit you well. There will be more contract work and more part-time work, with a growing proportion of self-employed people. It is in that way that jobs will be shared around, rather than by formal negotiation. Many firms, faced with the need to reduce their employed staff, have preferred to give some people part-time contracts for a fee, for a specified number of years, rather than pay them off altogether in a full-scale redundancy programme. That way, the organisation keeps some of the experience, and talents, and friends whom it has built up over the years, but at a reduced cost. It can even afford to pay a generous fee for the part-time work because of the saving in overheads. For the individual, if he is offered it, it is a less hazardous way into the rôle of a self-employed person. It is the experienced expert who is most likely to be offered this sort of alternative relationship with the organisation – someone in his fifties, in other words, who has a definable skill or expertise. Once again, it is the fifties generation who will be in the lead, like it or not.

More contract and more part-time work means more insecurity. Building workers, actors, journalists, and female outworkers have been the classically insecure and exploited people of our times. Will it change? The professions found a way to combine freedom and security by establishing and maintaining an effective closed shop. Solicitors, for example, control the entry routes into their profession and can then fix charges and, in theory, ensure that they are not overcrowded with new aspiring solicitors. Trades and occupations with a specific skill base, carpenters for instance, or electricians, could combine to operate a similar sort of guild. Many of us, however, do not work in an occupation which can be so precisely defined or fenced around. We shall inevitably be more exposed to the realities of the market place and will have to learn to look after our own interests. Traditionally, individuals in the 'open' occupations of writing, modelling, or broadcasting (for example), where anyone with pretensions to talent can apply for work, use an 'agent' to negotiate in their interests. There is an obvious opportunity for the idea of the 'agent' to expand to include all categories of the self-employed.

Will the employment agencies of today turn around and work for the individual not the organisation? Will new legislation come into being to fix the minimum conditions that have to be met by freelance contracts? Perhaps the biggest need is for more help for the self-employed to market their talents, goods, and services. It is *marketing* co-operatives which modern society needs, almost more than the production co-operatives which get all the attention.

THE MEANING OF WORK

Hans Selye, the authority on stress, writes:

'Work is a biological necessity. Just as our muscles become flabby and degenerate if not used, so our brain slips into chaos and confusion unless we constantly use it for some work that seems worthwhile to us.'

The question is not whether we should or should not work, but what kind of work suits us best.

A survey for the *Guardian* newspaper in December 1981 asked what were the main elements in job satisfaction. Top of the list came:

Personal freedom
Respect of colleagues
Learning something new
Challenge
Completing a project
Helping other people

Twenty-fourth on the list was money, seventeenth was security. They may have been deluding themselves or the *Guardian*, of course, but what they seem to be saying is that work provides them with the opportunity to fulfil themselves, to grow, and to work with and for others. That is another way of saying that work is essential to the full expression of our humanity.

Work has always provided men with their principal *structure for mattering*. We all need to *matter* to some people, to have their respect, to be able to contribute, to belong. The worst thing that can happen to anyone is to feel that they do not matter any more, to anyone, even themselves. Work, as Hans Selye and the *Guardian* survey agree, is not primarily about money but about mattering. It used to be the family which provided women with their principal structure for mattering, but for more and more women today it is clear that work is as important for them as it is for men.

'Work'? Or 'job'? Do the two words mean the same? Obviously not, for we all do some work, in the informal economy, which is not a job. Have we then done a vast disservice to society by letting ourselves think that work means jobs? We say 'there is no work available' meaning 'there are no jobs.' 'I can't live without work' may be true, but is 'I can't live without a job' so self-evidently true?

I suggest that there is an urgent need to redefine that word 'work' so that it means more than 'jobs'. Let us think of work as 'useful activity' instead of 'job'; we can then very readily distinguish three very different types of work with this broader meaning.

Job-work is the first and most obvious type. It is the conventional employment or self-employment.

Pocket-money work is a little different. It is work which we do for money, but for marginal money. We do not expect to make enough from it to cover *all* our expenses, only the expenses of that bit of work. If someone sells their surplus apples at the gate in the autumn, he does not expect to have to make enough to pay the rent but looks on the income as 'gravy' money, extra cash, or pocket money, and is grateful if it is enough to pay for the spray he used or the new ladder he had to buy. Job-work is supposed to earn us enough to pay for all we *need*, if not all we *want*. Pocket-money is extra. Much of the 'black economy' is pocket-money work, done in the evenings or the weekends to supplement the normal wage.

Gift-work is the work which is done for free, for ourselves, our families or our friends. The work which is done in the household economy, housework, gardening, or DIY is all gift-work. So, more obviously, is the work which we do as volunteers for some organisation. In a recent survey forty-two per cent of the people interviewed said they had done some sort of voluntary work in the last year and eighteen per cent had done six hours or more in the last week. There is a lot of it about.

The community scene
Opportunities for gift work
Tick the activities which are represented in your neighbourhood:

A festival
Playgroups
A youth club
A drama club
A choir or chorus
Evening classes
Football facilities
Swimming pool
Bowls
Information/advice centre
A 'small industries group'
A 'young enterprise group'
A 'job-swap' centre
A cinema or film club
Scouts, Guides, Brownies, Cubs
A local rock group
A folk club
A print workshop
A community magazine
Clubs for the disabled/
  housebound
Clubs for the mentally
  handicapped

Good local transport
  arrangements
A holiday playscheme
Allotments
A neighbourhood Law Centre
A women's group
A local environment concern
  group
A library
A meeting room/hall
A credit union
A street warden scheme
A housing action campaign
A street market
A parent/teacher association
A gingerbread group for single-
  parent families
A schools action group
An unemployment support group
A disco

_____ extra items
_____ extra items
_____ extra items
_____ extra items

How does your neighbourhood score?

30–35 Your community is alive and well – you shouldn't have much difficulty finding things to do.

20–30 Your community is waking up – you could help to move it along.

10–20 It's just about got the sleep out of its eyes.

0–10 Still pretty sleepy.

Adapted from G. Dauncey *The Unemployment Handbook*

If we look back to the list of what people wanted from work we can see that each type of work has something in its favour.

Pocket-money work scores well on personal freedom, learning something new, challenge, and completing a project.

Gift-work scores high on helping other people and offers opportunity for respect of colleagues and learning something new.

51

Job-work *could* offer opportunity for all, but is likely to be most valued for those two items ranked at the bottom of the list, money and security. Not everyone finds that job-work does measure up to its possibilities. Eighty per cent in the *Guardian* survey felt that they could contribute more to their organisation and a high number said that the job fell short of their original expectations. To get the most out of *work*, we need, perhaps, to think of a combination of all three types of work some time during our life. It does not have to be all at once. Typically there is a bit of pocket-money in youth (the newspaper round, odd jobs) which is then followed by job-work (if one is lucky). Later in life gift-work around the house and around the community begins to be more important. In the third age, gift-work and pocket-money could dominate. We should not be conned into thinking that only job-work is real work. The other two also have their strengths.

Pocket-money work

Buretire is an agency which seeks to find employment for people in their fifties or older who want 'occupation' rather than money. One man who had been an international banker tried working as a forecourt attendant but found it not very mentally stimulating and is now supervising a leisure centre at £60 a week.

Jobs that young people are loth to do, whatever the pay, are often acceptable to their elders. They don't mind opening up the newsagent's shop at 6.30 am or manning the telephone at a school for the handicapped from 5.30 to 10.30 pm. Older men and women can also be very helpful in passing on business contacts to new firms run by younger people.

Almost all the jobs which Buretire find are part-time, and their success is such that there are plans to open two hundred offices by 1983.

Reported by Mary Stott in *Ageing for Beginners*

In gift-work and pocket-money *you* are the crucial factor, what *you* can do, give, or make happen. You are no cog in a machine because you are the guts of whatever machine there is. If you sell or give your produce, your handiwork, or just your helping hands, it is very much a personal involvement you are making. There is also a directness about the relationship between you and the receiver or the customer which is a pleasing contrast with the inevitable remoteness of the big business system or the office bureaucracy. Pocket-money work, or gift work, is often what Schumacher called 'good work' combining, as it does, the opportunity to relate to people, to contribute and to create or express oneself. They have their drawbacks, of course. The first is money. It is no good relying on these forms of work for your main financial support. They are only possible when your overheads are taken care of in some way – by job-work, by a pension or savings. The second drawback can be a lack of structure. It is all very well to say 'do a bit of extra work on the side' or 'help out in the community' but it is not that easy to get started. There aren't many pocket-money job agencies, although one is described on page 52. Gift-work is rather better served if it is voluntary work you are interested in and Chapter 9 will give you a list of places and people to get in touch with, but it is still *you* who have to get started. It is no-one else's responsibility to drag you away from the television or the fire-side chair.

I suggest that it is in society's best interests for marginal-cost or pocket-money work to grow. If all work were to be charged out at its full costs a lot of tasks would be so expensive that they would never get done. It already happens. We have priced a lot of work out of existence. Streets and pavements are not cleaned as well or as often as they should be because it would cost too much. How many people clean their windows today, now that no-one can afford to pay a window cleaner? Who is painting out grafitti on our buildings, repairing broken fittings in high-rise blocks, answering the telephone after-hours at schools, surgeries, or clinics? Who is helping elderly shoppers with their bags from the supermarket, supervising children in break, running teenage clubs, planting shrubs and cutting grass along the highways, shovelling snow from the pavements? We could all compile our own list.

Many of these jobs, if marginally priced, that is done by people part-time who did not expect a full rate for the job, would once again be within the purchasing power of the householder or the local council. In our concern to get proper pay for all jobs we may have thrown the baby out with the bathwater, in that we have forced people to say 'if that's what it's going to cost then we won't do it at all'. Naturally, if pocket-money work is going to be attractive we must not penalise it with taxation. If it is seen as a taxable act to 'top up' your pension or your main earnings then no-one is going to bother, *or* they are going to do it and keep quiet about it, building up the black economy. We need to make pocket-money respectable, for the individual and for society.

It is important that much of this work is paid for, even if the pay is at marginal levels. If the employed sector of society needs work done they must expect to pay for it. At full cost this work could not be afforded, therefore let the market find a level of pocket-money payment which is attractive to people looking for marginal work. To expect all such work to be gift-work is in a sense to be scrounging on the goodwill of those who are out of work.

An alternative is to hand over more of the important and glamorous work to gift-work agencies. Life-boat crews and mountain rescue teams are gift-workers. In no way do they feel that society is scrounging on their time and talents. Rather it is an honour to serve. Is there more work of this nature which is worthwhile, of high standard and independent? Could the fire service again become voluntary in some of our smaller towns and villages where it is not a full-time requirement? Business and community leaders are beginning to combine to provide free advisory services to small businesses in their communities. The scope for increasing the professionalisation of voluntary work is discussed in Chapter 8, where I suggest that, in addition to the concept of 'helping others' which is so crucial, the voluntary organisations can give an individual both training and professional qualifications, thus making this form of gift-work even more useful than it already is to the individual and to society. To use gift-work, however, to do the *chores of society* seems to me to be exploiting charity.

If we do move to a society in which the three types of work are both more acceptable and more blended into one life-style we may find that men are beginning to adopt the kind of life-styles which women have traditionally followed or been stuck with, just at the time when women have started to crack the male domination of job-work. It could be an ironic paradox, as men run into the kind of problems which women have long confronted.

Full-time job-work for women is now a fact of life although the attitudes of men, and women, have not fully caught up with it. However, full-time jobs have confronted many women with an agonising choice – a choice that men have not usually had to face, because for women family is at the core of their lives, while for most men it is at the edge.

'It never felt like I had a *real* choice. It just seemed the right thing to do, you know, to take the job that was nearer, even if it wasn't as good. That way, I would be able to keep the home going without too much trouble.' Job-work had to be combined with gift-work at home, or in the end changed into what was, effectively, pocket-money work.

Part-time work was one way out of that dilemma, particularly once the children were at school. But part-time work has not been serious work *up to now*. Anything less than the 3× 48 type jobs were just playing at work, often for pocket-money. If fees and out-work become more common in the second half of the eighties it should work greatly to the advantage of women because they have had so much more experience of blending work and home than their husbands. On top of that, much of the work will be of the sort that requires brains, eyes, and fingers – not muscles. The traditional physical superiority of the male will not any longer be an advantage when work consists of sitting at a bench or in front of a television screen for most of the day.

Will we then see more house husbands and more wives in mainstream job-work? Maybe we will not face such a universal rôle reversal but a redefinition of 'work' will certainly make it easier to blend the traditional rôles.

Who gets the job-work

A senior official of a white collar trade union recently told the Equal Opportunities Commission that his job was to ensure that as many men got and kept jobs as possible and not to let women take men's jobs away.

The Dutch Government, however, sees a huge growth in part-time work as one way to provide work for women in families, disabled people, and other disadvantaged groups, while at the same time offering to young people a way of combining some work with their studies and to older people a phased progress towards retirement.

In Gröningen in Holland, in 1980, the post office union and the local management negotiated an agreement which got rid of half of the part-time work-force. The evicted part-timers banded together, picketed the post office and forced government intervention. The union reversed its position and became a supporter of part-time work.

Reported by David Clutterbuck in the *Guardian*, 4 November 1981

LEISURE

Leisure is the other side of all this work.

But what is leisure?

Paul Evans and Fernando Bartolome in their book *Must Success Cost So Much?* suggest four different views of leisure. Which is yours?

1 Leisure as recovery – passing time. Television is the most popular 'pastime'. Others are similar non-activities, like snoozing, drinking and chatting in the pub, or mild activities such as doing jobs around the house. Most of these activities are solitary for conversation appears to inhibit recovery. Tired people don't want to talk. 'Don't bother Daddy, he's tired'.

2 Leisure as relaxation – getting rid of tensions. Participation in some form of sport or some very active hobby helps to clear the mind of other things, as well as tuning up the body. In comparison with other groups, managers and professional people do a lot of active leisure, perhaps because of the stress they feel in their jobs.

3 Leisure as family investment. 'The family that plays together stays together' is the concept behind this use of leisure. Activities are planned which involve the whole family. Camping, family holidays, barbecues, and picnics, family games all fall into this category. This form of leisure is of course, much more common when the family is young.

4 Leisure as personal development. This form of leisure takes in hobbies and interests which could often prove the basis of a second career. Men and women in their twenties and thirties have little time or interest in this form of leisure. It becomes more relevant in later life.

Different societies also had different concepts of leisure. To the Greeks leisure was the point and purpose of life. Necessary work should be done by slaves. Governments, wars, and schools were too important to be left to slaves but were still not things to take too seriously. Great men rose above all that and concentrated on the best way to enjoy their leisure – in conversation, in sport, in meditation or learning. It was a serious business, leisure, to the Greeks.

The Romans had ideas more akin to those of today. Leisure was self-indulgence – a reward for one's labours. It was a philosophy which tended to produce corruption, or at least indolence, at the top, caricatured in Nero's life and times, fiddling both literally and metaphorically while Rome burnt. At the bottom it led to a policy for keeping the people quiet by an endless diet of 'bread and circuses' or free leisure opportunities.

Luther and Calvin changed all that. Work was what it was all about, work was our opportunity to share in God's creation and earn a passport to wherever paradise was. Great men needed no leisure. Weak men needed it to restore their flagging energies. Leisure therefore was corrupting when excessive and should be unnecessary except as rest and relaxation. This was the Protestant work ethic.

In 1981 work took up less than ten per cent of the time of all people in the United Kingdom. More precisely, work took up nine per cent and leisure thirty-one per cent. The biggest slice goes in sleep (thirty-seven per cent). These figures are arrived at by aggregating the living time of all people living in the UK and then totting up the total time spent in work, leisure and other activities and converting to percentages. This is the conclusion of Bill Martin and Sandra Mason who have completed a major research study of leisure.

In the early 1970s, they say, an important milestone was passed when the average full-time worker began to spend more of his or her year at leisure than at work. This trend they see increasing, as 'time' becomes more important in the bargains people make in work and life.

Leisure and Work: The Choices for 1991 and 2001 for Leisure Consultants

It is interesting to complete one's own work/leisure breakdowns, having first decided what those two words mean.

How does your week divide up?

WHAT TYPE OF LEISURE WILL FIT THE 1980s

Leisure as 'recovery' or 'relaxation' after work is an insult to those who have little or no work. We may therefore expect to see this type of leisure increasingly concentrated on those who are in the midst of full-time job-work. Family leisure, likewise, will be increasingly impor-tant to young parents with growing children who will revel in longer holidays and weekends, but has little relevance to people whose fami-lies have grown up and gone. For those contemplating the tailing-off of job-work and looking for leisure opportunities which may provide an alternative 'structure for mattering' it is the fourth type of leisure which has most meaning. Would it be too anachronistic to find the views of the Greeks becoming relevant again nearly two and a half thousand years later? Rita Sidebottom, writing in her late fifties, gives one woman's approach to leisure in her third ago, in the quotation which follows. Not everyone will share her interest in industrial archaeology or her talents for writing. Some will turn travel into an opportunity for learning. Others will turn collectors while still others may find their home in religion.

Life and leisure in the Third Age

'For the first time I've got time to stand and stare. The pleasure of wak-ing up naturally instead of the aching tiredness of dragging myself out of bed at 6.30 am every morning; being able to watch television at night without falling asleep; the pleasure of walking around looking at shops instead of a mad rush on a Saturday; to shop in midweek when the assistants have time to be pleasant; to sit in the precinct and have a chat. Funny, I never knew there were so many lonely people about. It's a new world.

I've got time now to attend more of Stockport's Historical Society's lectures, and to spend on my special interest of industrial archaeology. Perhaps I'll get down to some research on one of my pet subjects – old mills.

I study basic English one day a week at the Literacy and Language and Numeracy Unit at Stockport – I still have hopes of becoming a writer. The help and encouragement I receive is wonderful. I still have a lot to learn about nouns, verbs, adjectives and the like. I thought I would have been the oldest one there, surrounded by teenagers. It wasn't like that at all – most of the women were in their thirties and forties – mostly mid-thirties – but no men at all in an English class.

I find the writing comes easy. I also find I can contribute something to the class, with my experiences of life which were numerous and varied – and being an out-going person I talk easily on most subjects. So it's a happy time in class. Different from when I was at school.

I've written a couple of short stories and a few short scripts for televi-sion – all rejected. My son keeps telling me Hemingway had his first

Cont.

manuscript rejected twenty-five times – which doesn't help much but I keep going. At the moment I'm working on an article about how the sewers came into being in Manchester in the 1830s and 1840s. I'm surprised how quickly the day passes. There just isn't time enough. When I was at work I promised myself I would have a good old sort out of cupboards and sheds when I retired – but I still haven't got round to it.

If it's a nice day we take a packed lunch and go into the country, picking blackberries. I remember the time we used to use that as an excuse, but now at our age we pick 'em. *I'm enjoying the late summer of my life very much. The harvest has been bountiful. Long may it continue.'*

Rita Sidebottom writing in The *Guardian*, 24 October 1981

I have spelt out the leisure options at some length in order to make the point that leisure is not only relaxation and hobbies. A life with a lot of leisure is not necessarily a lazy or a purposeless one. But even the Greeks did *some* work. Leisure is the counterpart of work. A life of leisure and no work would be an incomplete life. Job-work, as I have argued, is not the whole of work, neither is leisure the whole of life. We need work, of one type or another, to make the most of leisure.

A man in Doncaster was talking about the hobbies his wife was trying to interest him in, after his redundancy. 'But you need a free mind for things like that,' he said. What did he mean? He meant, I believe, that leisure as personal development had to be taken seriously. If you have no work you can't get down to leisure. That's the rebuff to those who see a 'leisure society' as the answer to one's dilemmas. More leisure, yes. Total leisure, no. First, let us redefine work and make sure that everyone has his or her due share of it – then we can concentrate on leisure.

THE TWO SCENARIOS

The optimist can see a world where words like retirement, redundancy and unemployment lose their meaning. It is not impossible. After all, we only started using 'unemployment' in the last century, and redundancy is from a much more recent vintage. Why might they go away? Not because everyone will be employed for all of their life, but because the words won't make sense if we redefine 'work' in the broader ways suggested, if work and leisure and life get more woven together again.

Retirement, unemployment and redundancy only make sense in job-work terms. Self-employed people do not, cannot, become unemployed or redundant (only bankrupt!). Housewives don't retire, they just stop. Farmers may talk of hard years, of slowing down or cutting down, but never of being redundant. One farmer in his seventies, commenting on the theme of this book, said 'your seventies are no different from the fifties or the thirties; you do the same things only slower'.

The optimist's scenario sees work and leisure and adequate money for all, with lots of room for individual variation.

The pessimist sees the factories staffed by sophisticated engineers, robots and electronic maintenance men and the offices run by capable part-timers, with the more disciplined and better educated looking after their terminals at home. What then happens to the rest of us? Do we sit, propped up by the dole, in front of a micro-wave oven perched on top of a television set boring ourselves to death, or watching endless dials on some monitor board? I watched a man watching a machine putting mints into a tube. That was his job – to watch in case the machine skipped a mint. It never did. Is that what work will be in the new age?

Which scenario is more likely? Can we make the optimistic one into a self-fulfiling prophecy? I hope so.

CHAPTER FOUR

TAKING STOCK OF YOURSELF

How about ourselves in the fifties?

A businessman's stock is his raw material for the future. Every so often, he counts it, and values it, to see where he stands. Why should it be any different for individuals? Why are we so strangely reluctant to look at what we've got within us and what we might do with it? 'To take stock. But that's illegal!' said a friend. He was joking, deliberately misinterpreting that word 'take', but humour can be a cover for deeper truths. There is, in Britain, a deep distrust of people who are turned-in on themselves and an abiding suspicion that too much analysis leads to paralysis. These instincts are sensible, but, carried too far, they can mean that we end up as strangers even to ourselves. Do you really know who you are? How would you value your personal 'stock'? Where are you heading in life?

As we approach the third age of life these questions get more pressing. We can no longer skip them on the pretext that we have not lived long enough to know the answers. Consciously or unconsciously most of us worked for our parents in our early life – to prove them right or to prove them wrong. By the time we are fifty, we have grown up and are living for ourselves. There is no-one left, if there ever was, to direct or influence our destinies or to protect us, or to be blamed. We, and we only, are now in charge. It must be time to take stock a little more seriously, of ourselves, where we come from, who we are, what we've got and where we are going to. Businessmen are required by law to take stock at regular intervals. We have no such built in reminders, and often wait for one of the emotional triggers mentioned in Chapter 1 to set us thinking. We could however do it a little more deliberately and in a more leisurely fashion.

WHO ARE YOU?

Ask this question of anybody and they will first respond with a name. This won't normally get them very far so they will go on to tell you what they do, what their occupation is or their job. 'I'm a secretary', they'll say, or 'I work on the railways' or 'I look after the family'. That gets them through the introductions in the pub, it helps others to put them into some sort of box so that they know how to relate to them and the kind of things to talk about, but it doesn't tell us very much about them as persons unless we assume that all secretaries are the same, and all railway-workers too.

Are women different from men in this? Dr Lillian Rubin was researching the attitudes of women in the USA to mid-life and asked a wide range of women to respond to this question. 'Who are you?' None of the women answered the question by referring to their work rôles even when those rôles were important and successful, but spoke instead of their family or home. No one said 'I'm a teacher', 'I'm a secretary' or 'I'm a seamstress'. One woman, questioned about this said, 'I don't really know why I didn't say anything about my work. It's certainly very important to me; I like what I do. I think maybe it has something to do with how I see myself as a whole person. Yes, that's it. Being a lawyer is what I *do*; you asked me who I *am*.' In contrast she asked thirty-five men to respond to the same question and everyone started his answer by mentioning his job.

How would you answer the question? Better than imagining an answer, try writing it down. Picture yourself having to explain who you are to a sympathetic and anonymous stranger. It was an Irishman who said 'How do I know what I think until I hear what I say?' We could amend it to read 'How do I know who I am until I hear what I tell someone else?'

Joe Lutz and Harry Ingham created a diagram which they called the Johari window to explain the problem we have in knowing ourselves.

The Johari window

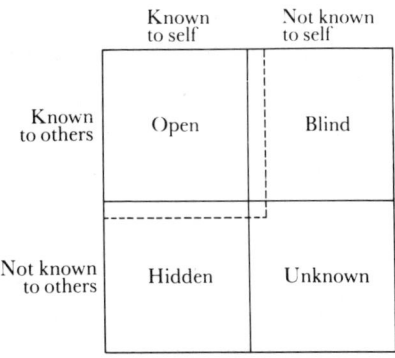

There is a part that is our common identity (open), which would include our job or rôle, and some other facts about us like our age, sex and physical appearance. Then there is the hidden 'us' which we know but do not reveal, and that side of us (blind) which others know and we do not. Lastly there is the unknown, the unconscious part of us.

The more we can push back the boundaries of the open square the more we shall be in charge of ourselves and our life. The tendency, unfortunately, in times of stress or crisis is to shrink into ourselves narrowing down that open square. The suggestions which follow are intended to help you to pull up the blinds on yourself, so that you can take stock more efficiently.

Have you ever considered writing your autobiography? No, one does not have to be famous to have an autobiography – everyone could have that. It is just that only a few get printed and published. My father-in-law started to write his towards the end of his life, as a memento for his family. It was fascinating to read and, I have little doubt, fascinating for him to write, as he dredged up bits of himself from the past.

An autobiography is a lot of work. There are other ways of discovering the patterns in one's life and of identifying the critical events which shaped one's career. The exercise described below is one of them, but to be effective it needs to be done with other people who can share *their* lives with you. Preferably these people should be more of those sympathetic strangers, but failing these a group of friends at the same stage in life will provide an adequate sounding board. Talking to yourself is easier, but less useful, because we skate around the difficult questions or omit bits of us which others can perceive.

Take a pencil and a piece of paper and draw a line, any sort of line, to represent your life from birth to death. When you have done that then mark with a cross where you are on the line right now. Do this before you read any further.

You may have drawn a simple straight line, but as you think about it a bit more you will almost certainly find that you want to draw a line a bit like the one below.

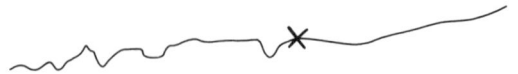

What you have, in effect, done is to draw a graph. Along the bottom you could measure off 'time' in years. The interesting question is 'What is the vertical axis measuring?' What are you going up and down on? Is it happiness, or success, or money?

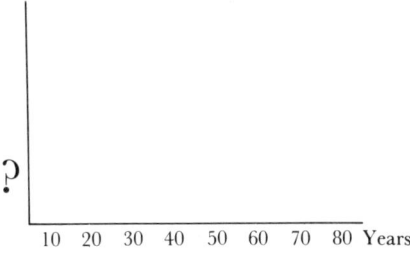

Most people, when they draw the lines, do not really know the answer to that question. They just know that there are good times and bad times. The point is to understand what it was that you valued in the good times and what you learnt from the bad times.

To find this out talk through your life-line with the others in the group, if you have found one. Remember, this line is YOUR life. Your recollection of events may not be strictly accurate. That does not matter. It is how YOU remember them that is important, because it is on YOU that the events made their mark. Even if you only talk to yourself about your life-line you may discover that you bring out things you had long put away in your mind but which might be very important.

The bit of the line beyond the cross (where you are now) is interesting. How long is it? Is it going up or down? Does it look as if it was drawn with certainty or does it waver a little? This last bit of the line we draw with very little conscious thought because it has no facts underlying it. It has therefore to be our very intuitive feelings about the general tenor or feel for our life in the years ahead.

Here are some questions which may help you to look at the life-line of yourself or others:

1 What do the turning-points have in common?
   Are they all to do with work, or family, or money?

2 What sorts of events were crises for you?

3 How did you get out of them? Is there a pattern?

4 What were peak experiences for you?

5 What kinds of risks do you take?

6 Did you prefer the plateaux or the slopes?

7 What does this tell you about the sort of person you are?

63

Life-lines I have known

All the way home is downhill. Could she really mean that?

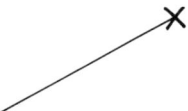

Does he expect to die at tea-time?

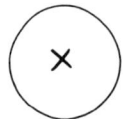

He never did want to be connected with his life.

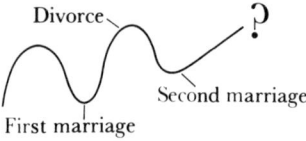

Is she telling herself something?

IS THERE A MID-LIFE CRISIS?

Biographies and life-lines, even if done over a drink, are very conscious and deliberate ways of answering part of the WHO AM I? question. The process can be much more tortuous and tortured, triggered off by one of the events listed in Chapter 1, such as the death of a parent, divorce or redundancy. In the opening stanzas of *The Divine Comedy*, Dante, in his late thirties, which is equivalent of today's fifties, expressed it dramatically:

'In the middle of the journey of our life, I came to myself within a dark wood, where the straight way was lost. Ah, how hard it is to tell of that wood, savage and harsh, and dense, the thought of which renews my fear. So bitter is it that death is hardly more.'

If there is a 'mid-life crisis', this is it, the eventual 'meeting with oneself', and all the questions which that arouses. For myself, this meeting happened at my father's funeral and took four years to work through. In retrospect, much of the trauma could have been avoided if I had known what was happening and could have done it all rather more consciously. It may be, of course, that we all have to learn the hard way.

Stephanie wrote to us when she heard we were preparing this book: 'I was a lone parent for nineteen years. My children and I were a closeknit warm and living nucleus of four in a big, untidy flat which seemed spilling over with people and activity, and despite being broke too often, being in a crisis too often, and stressed all of the time, I felt at the hub of our tiny universe, rich and fulfilled, when suddenly it all began to break up, spontaneously, from several directions at once. One child went to university, another to America, and my ex-husband lost his job and needed the money from the sale of the flat we lived in (his). Confronted by the dissolution of my universe – the fall into chaos – I did the most extraordinary thing.

I took my share of the proceeds of the sale and bought a totally derelict farmhouse in the remotest part of the Cambrian mountains, isolating myself from the human race for a period of three years.

I had two hazily perceived motivations. The first was that I had long had self-sufficiency, goats and geese and at-one-with-nature dreams which I now intended to fulfil. The other was a more obscure unexpressed longing to 'find myself' which to my semi-mystical cast of mind meant the obligatory 'forty days and nights in the desert' which I proposed to extend to the rest of my life for lack of any alternative. Oh yes, and of course I was going to draw and paint and write and enter into the fulfilment of my own creativity! I had absolutely no insight whatever into what I was doing.

Phew, this was strong stuff! I was catapulted from the bosom of my family into a derelict house at the top of an inaccessible mountain, suffering from unrecognised 'involutional melancholia' (the now discredited definition of menopausal depression) and unacknowledged bereavement. I flung myself recklessly into re-building, undertaking tasks far beyond my strength, but *anything* to keep out the grief battering at my door.

After two years I had a nervous breakdown. My old dog, last link with my happy days, had to be put down and the great rampart of the dam inside me cracked – and broke. I was washed away in a storm of grief, drowning in bereavement and despair.

A year after that, and three years after I had isolated myself, I slipped one Sunday afternoon quietly into possession of myself. The search was over. The insight came unbidden, and without fanfare.

It was a weekend, like so many others, when my children had come on an eagerly-anticipated visit. Much water had passed under the bridge, their visits now were much rarer than initially, all three were

Cont.

entrenched in their own lives. At three o'clock on Sunday afternoon they packed up their cars and one by one they rolled away. I sat on the sofa, picked up the paper, but instead of looking at it, I looked at the despair that was threatening me. And I said 'No'. I put my paper down and looked carefully and wonderingly at the past three years; no, decade; no, lifetime. And I saw that my whole emotional life had been a *reaction* to others. And I didn't want it any more because it had been damaging, painful, often inappropriate. I wanted to *act*, from my own self, which I now perceived to be calmly and tranquilly alive and well and living behind and below and around this monstrous and unacceptable, conditioned and unreal set of reactions. So I sloughed off the reactions and slipped into myself softly, as a swimmer slips gratefully into the open sea.

Insight, revelation, is always like that, quiet, calm and undramatic. It waits where knowledge ends, activity ceases, and the programmed tapes of the mind are turned off. Yet I do believe you have searched up to its very door before it comes upon you, unawares, like grace itself.'

Two researchers in the north-east of England (Hepworth and Featherstone) have suggested that if there is a mid-life crisis, it is often a silent crisis. They tell of a harbour worker who suddenly disappeared from home. Because he was quiet and inoffensive his family could not understand what had gone wrong. When he returned a few days later, and told them that reorganisation at work and a missed promotion had got him down, all was apparently forgotten and forgiven. A silent crisis suddenly revealed and quickly buried again as if it had never happened.

Quite obviously some people, who have sunk a lot of their identity into their work or career, can reach some sort of crunch point in the middle of that second age of working. They may have done well enough to have got what they wanted only to find that they didn't then want what they had got, or they may have had to come to terms with the reality that they were never going to achieve what they had set their heart on. Either way, mid-life for these people can provide one of the triggers which set off a period of taking stock. The more committed to your work, the more likely it will be that you will have, or have had, this experience. The 'work' for many people can be raising a family, and many a parent has found the departure of the children a big trigger event. 'What do I do now?' 'What am I working for?'

Do not however feel deprived if you have not been through a mid-life crisis. It is not inevitable, necessary or desirable. Perhaps it is a twentieth-century phenomenon, a consequence of the importance which we have heaped upon work as a source of our identity.

THE TALENT STOCK

You, however, are more than a biography or a life-line or even a mid-life crisis. You are also a bundle of talents, a clutch of hope and ambitions, a bank of assets, a being full of passions and personality. Someone once suggested that by the time he dies the average individual has only discovered one quarter of all his talents. It is an unproveable idea but it has the ring of truth about it. Unfortunately, whenever we assess ourselves, we tend to think of the talents we don't have rather than the ones we do have, discovered and undiscovered. The form provided below is one way of getting yourself thinking positively about your 'stock'. If you use it, do so honestly with no false modesty. Remember too, that there are some 'negative' assets, like never being really ill. When you have done the list, ask a good friend if there is anything he or she could add (not subtract) to it.

Stock check

1 What do you enjoy doing most?
   1 _____
   2 _____
   3 _____

2 What do people admire you for?
   1 _____
   2 _____
   3 _____

3 What things do you do best?
   1 _____
   2 _____
   3 _____

4 What are your *practical* skills? (car maintenance, cooking, etc.)
   1 _____
   2 _____
   3 _____

5 What are your *creative* skills? (telling stories, designing, etc.)
   1 _____
   2 _____
   3

6 What are your skills with *people*? (managing, listening, encouraging, etc.)
   1 _____
   2 _____
   3 _____

Cont.

7 What are your *intellectual* skills? (analysing, organising, thinking, etc.)

1 _____

2 _____

3 _____

8 What are your *natural assets?* (health, good looks, charm, personality, etc.)

1 _____

2 _____

3 _____

9 What are your principal *material assets?* (home, car, job, etc.)

1 _____

2 _____

3 _____

If you sold up everything, what would you be worth in £s.

4 _____

10 Who are your principal *people assets?* (spouse, children, friends, etc.)

1 _____

2 _____

3 _____

Now

11 What are your principal weaknesses?

1 _____

2 _____

3 _____

And

12 What would you do if you had your time once again?

1 _____

2 _____

3 _____

Questions 11 and 12 in the stock check are important. We all have weaknesses which are often only the opposite side of our strengths. That professors are absent-minded is truer than you might think because their minds are, or should be, on other things. Creative people can be shy and buttoned-up in their relations with other people. On the other hand hearty people are so busy projecting themselves that they can be insensitive to others. It might be a mistake to try too hard to correct some weaknesses because you then interfere with the thing they are the opposite of. Turn the artist into the life and soul of the party and you may ruin his art. Nevertheless, it is important that you are aware of your weaknesses and make provision for them.

Question 12 is an invitation to dream. There is still time to be all that you wanted to be. Many a businessman who 'takes stock' will discover that he over-invested in some areas of his business and neglected others. So it is with life. In our preoccupation with survival and with getting over the hurdles of job, marriage, and family, we may have neglected some aspects of life which are crying out for investment. Do not hide them away any longer – bring them in from the shadows, and for once forget your innate modesty and humility. Be as arrogant as you dare! Autobiographies, life-line and stock-check are mirror devices – ways of looking at oneself. We have to remember, however, that mirrors distort. We all have our own ways of looking in the mirror so that we see the side of ourselves which we want to see. That is why I have stressed the need for the sympathetic listener. Ironically, family and friends are not the best listeners. They know us too well, or think they do, and will tell us what they think we want to hear or what fits their image of us. That does not help us to draw the hidden parts of our personality.

Families and friends can indeed be part of the difficulty because we may have given some of them the rôle of judges. We have to ask ourselves whom we have set up, unconsciously, to be our judges because we all have them tucked away in the back of our minds. Arthur Grimble, in *A Pattern of Islands*, felt that he was being perpetually judged by the Uncles, 'meaning every man jack of your father's generation, uncle or not, who cared to take you by the arm.'

Katherine Whitehorn tells how she always felt her life was being picked over by her mother's school friends. For others it is those 'old school friends' themselves, or one's colleagues at work, or the people next door. I myself was continually bringing back little gobbets of success to my mother until I discovered that she was only interested in my domestic life and personal happiness. Who do we work for? Who are the neighbours we mean when we say 'what would the neighbours say?' Who are the people 'back home' whose approval we really want?

Part of growing up is releasing oneself from the self-imposed judges and putting more relevant ones in their place, thus taking responsibility for setting one's own standards and aspirations. We ought to be able to do it in the fifties but the past can keep a strong hold. Is that why we occasionally need to run away and hide, in order to escape from our judges? Autobiographies, life-lines and stock-checks may sound gimmicky or tedious or artificial, but their purpose is to help you separate yourself, consciously, from the grip of the 'others' in your life, so that you are fully in charge of yourself and of your life. The sympathetic stranger, whether you meet him or her on a holiday somewhere, in the counsellor's office, or in the pub, can be a better listener than a closer friend, because he does not judge.

Write it down, too, if you can possibly find the time. Writing, like the prospect of hanging, concentrates the mind wonderfully. I shied away from all such exercises for a long time but when I was eventually bullied or coaxed into doing them they helped enormously to pull my true self out of the shadows.

Growing up at fifty

Many of us carry the luggage of our childhood well into middle-age. Growing up means getting rid of the luggage so that you can be truly oneself. For many, that does not happen until the fifties.

Harry was the child of quarrelling parents. His father could not hold down a job and they lived in a succession of seedy hotel rooms, lodgings and friends' spare rooms. His mother was unfaithful to his father so frequently that from the age of four his father slept in Harry's room and lectured him on morality and ethics before he went to sleep each night. Harry grew up to have an obsession about security, about cleanliness and about fidelity. *He* was never going to move job or house. Cutlery had to be wiped before eating. Crumbs and stains were horrors. His wife was allowed no friends or life of her own. Inevitably, these obsessions brought problems to his growing family and the prospect of separation if not divorce. Just in time, Harry was helped to see how he was compensating for a youth that was long past, burdening others with his childhood problems, the luggage of his youth. Slowly, he began to get rid of that luggage, to let other parts of himself show through. He began to grow up.

Sheila was an only child of a father who had very much wanted a son. Sheila adored her father and tried endlessly at school and afterwards to please him. She was a determined career girl and cared little for anything except the things which helped her on her path to her chosen career in the Civil Service. At the age of fifty-three she had a successful if not spectacular career, but her father died and she at the same time realised that she was not going to rise any farther in the service. Then it was that she began to reflect on all the things she had not done, the girl and the woman, even the wife and the mother, which she had not been, in her determination to be the son her father wanted. Now that he was no longer around she was free to be herself, not the person her father wanted. At fifty-three she had grown up.

We don't all carry around such heavy luggage from our past as these two, but there is usually some of it to get rid of before we can be truly ourselves.

WHAT KIND OF PERSON ARE YOU?

As well as a past and a collection of talents and assets, we also have a personality. If the secret of the third age is finding a niche or niches to suit us, then we must not neglect to take account of the kind of person we are. The study of personality is a quagmire into which it would not be sensible to step in this short book, but it may help to match yourself against some of the pictures of personality which the theorists have invented. I am not going to provide any questionnaires or personality tests, but will simply describe the pictures and their implications and leave you to make any connections with yourself that you please. If you want to go into it further you should consult a trained psychologist or psycho-therapist.

I have found three different classifications to be helpful in their own ways in helping me to decide on the appropriate niches in life.

1 Are you an *extrovert* or an *introvert*?

You are almost certainly a bit of both, but probably more one than the other. It was the Swiss psychoanalyst Jung who made the distinction, describing the extrovert as the outgoing personality, taking an active interest in everything around him, wanting to be involved with people and things. The introvert is more preoccupied with his own internal affairs, preferring to observe rather than initiate, to contemplate rather than to act. He may well appear shy in comparison with the gregarious extrovert. The extrovert likes attention and activity, the introvert preferring the quiet life.

Since we are all bits of both, the extrovert can, on occasion, become withdrawn, contemplating what is going on inside himself, and the introvert can push himself into social situations if he has to.

Most people have a pretty shrewd idea of which camp they belong to. It is very important that they realise there is not a good and a bad aspect to this question. It is not better to be an extrovert than an introvert, or the other way round. Both have their advantages and their snags.

If you know which you are can you shape your life accordingly? An introvert will not enjoy life as a publican nor will he be very successful as a salesman although the solitary aspects of the job may appeal. An extrovert should think twice about buying himself or herself a house in the country with only the birds to talk to. On the other hand, he or she would be more likely to go out and meet the neighbours.

I am writing this book because I am an introvert who wishes to be more of an extrovert! I want to communicate with people, to enter into their lives and their problems and to nudge society along a little. But introverts are shy, do not mix easily and shun conflict. It is easier therefore to write to people than to address them directly, and so I have adapted my way of living to suit what I came to recognise was one part of my personality.

71

2 Are you a feeling, thinking, or acting person?

Another classification pulls together these three aspects of each of our characters. Put them at the corners of a triangle and imagine each corner to have a magnet pulling towards them. Where would you end up? Not right in any one corner but probably more towards one than the other.

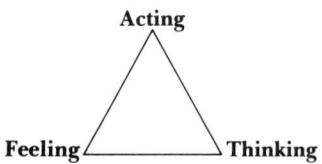

Where would you like to be?

People who like jumping into action don't always want to spare too much time thinking about it first. Sometimes, too, they can be insensitive. But thinkers can spend so much time analysing the situation that the problem solves itself before they get round to acting. Few of us are completely centred in the triangle. Which way do you incline? Is the part you play at work, or at home, the right one for you? Have you come to terms with where you are in the triangle or are you always wishing you were in another corner. The sensitive, quiet, thoughtful, person can long to be the Action Man of the family, but in practice he never makes it. Does he then think of himself as a failure or does he rejoice in his sensitivity and thoughtfulness? Women are often pushed into the Feeling corner against their will, because society assumes that that is where women naturally belong, yet then expects them to be equally good for Action. By the time you have reached your fifties, you ought to have come to terms with reality and worked out which situations suit you best.

3 Which Greek god do you take after?

Another classification, developed by myself for use in organisations, looks at some other dimensions of our personality, illustrated by four of the Greek gods.

ZEUS, as king of the gods, is interested in power, in making things happen, and quickly. He rules by thunderbolt and showers of gold, is intuitive rather than logical, likes or dislikes people quickly, which is important because he works largely through his own Mafia. He is a great entrepreneur, or fixer, or old-fashioned boss. His word goes and you notice when he is around. You could call him an extrovert and he is certainly a man of action.

APOLLO is the logical god, believing in rules and discipline and order. His followers like routine, security rather than excitement, and prefer things to be written down so that they know where they stand. There has to be a right way of doing things and it should be followed. The system is important to them. Everything and everyone has their place in a well-ordered life. Planning, budgets, and formal procedures are important to Apollonians.

ATHENA is the only female god in the group, chosen because she stands for wisdom, creativity, and leadership in battle. She looked after Ulysses and his adventurous gang. Her followers are interested in the challenge of new situations, but they like to work in groups, democratic groups. They get bored by routine, and like to combine their skills with others in order to get the best results. They are gregarious and good with people. Advertising agencies, consulting firms, and voluntary organisations, tend to use Athenian groups. Athena happens to be female but that does not mean that all women are Athenians, far from it – although the mixture of creativity and collaboration for which she stands is well-suited to many women.

DIONYSUS is the fourth god. He is the god of wine but also the god who stands for the individual and the right of the individual to do his or her own thing. The individualist, often the introvert individualist, is typically a Dionysian. Content to work on his own, resentful of bureaucracy or bosses, he or she may be a craftsman, an artist, a researcher, or a long-distance lorry-driver.

Which is your God? Different gods suit different occupations. Apollonians enjoy the structure and routine of organisations. For them the informal economy is a threatening place. If you are going to spend a lot of your time alone you will enjoy it more if you are a Dionysian, but you will be able to earn your living only if you have some saleable skill. Home-workers need to be Dionysian at heart. Athenians love working with other people, particularly on projects. The voluntary world is often a haven for them, but so are the work groups of small organisations, or the clubs of friends. Zeus people like to run things, as long as they can be in charge.

We are all a mix of all four gods, but usually one or other of them predominates. It is interesting, as well as fun, to see how these different personalities tend to run their homes and families in quite different ways. There are Apollonian families which run by routine, Zeus families where one parent lays down the law, often a changing law, Athenian families where group decisions are what matters, and everything becomes a family project, and, finally, Dionysian families where everyone does his own thing – which is hard on the child with an Apollonian need for structure.

WHAT'S YOUR LIFE ALL ABOUT?

'When in doubt, man loses himself in activity.' In our first two ages, those of growing and of working, we have often lost ourselves in busyness, swamped in other people's agendas. Those 'other' people may be at work – bosses, colleagues, customers; or at home – children, parents, husbands or wives. There wasn't really the time, or even the need, to worry about the point of it all – running in the race was hard enough, without thinking what the race was all for. But as we get older the question starts to loom more urgently. After all, there is no use listing all our talents and assets unless we know what it is we want to use them for.

From the observations of people at work, an American psychologist, Abraham Maslow, suggested that we were motivated by five needs in life which he listed as:

Physical   the need to eat, drink, and stay alive
Safety   the need to be secure
Belonging   the need to belong to a group of others
Esteem   the need to be valued and respected, to have status
Self-realisation the need to fulfil yourself

He further suggested that the order in which these needs were linked was important, because the second need did not come into force until the first was satisfied. We don't care about status when we are starving, nor about self-fulfilment when we've just become redundant and no longer belong anywhere.

Where are you on Maslow's ladder? If life has worked out all right you should have satisfied the first four needs and be working on the last one of self-realisation. A crisis at work or in the family may, however, have pulled you back as one of the earlier needs suddenly becomes unsatisfied again and demands recognition. Divorce can throw us right back on our uppers, worried about shelter and money in a way that radically upsets our priorities. Maslow would say that these needs have to be put to rights before you can move on to other priorities. It is interesting that communities like monasteries or convents try to take care of all the first four needs through the institution so that everyone can get on with the difficult task of self-realisation, or, as they would put it, getting closer to God.

Most people in their fifties will have managed without the monastery or convent. They will have got themselves to that fifth stage by their own efforts. Indeed, it is getting there that may actually be the cause of the mysterious mid-life crisis, because self-realisation is a difficult, intangible thing to get a hold of. What does it mean and how do you measure it? The answer will be different for everyone because each one of us has to start with a proper understanding of the self that we want to 'realise' or fulfil. No wonder many people are happier working away at the earlier needs which can be more easily understood and measured. In Maslow's terms the challenge of the fifties is the challenge of self-realisation, because the other needs are disposed of, hopefully for ever. Certainly that is the way many people see it.

Two experiences of change

John 'You can only get the best out of life by experiencing the depths of despair and the heights of delight. It is the struggle in life that brings the greatest rewards. I feel that job security can rob you of something, and it is bound to rub off on your private life. I've been unemployed now for twelve months and it's good, it's good because it forces you to organise yourself. I've turned into a DIY man and I find that I appreciate things much more, like birds and nature and people, because I've got more time and energy. I'm very pleased about it, but make no mistake, you've got to work at it, in order to justify your existence. I'm more mature than I was, plus the fact that my family are growing up now and I can see the end of my family commitments. I don't need so much money now, because I can fill my life with the things that don't cost money. Life is getting more eventful. I travel hopefully. You've got to plan for life continuing for a long, long time.'

Eileen 'At the age of fifty-seven I found it a very hard decision to make, to retire after forty-two years of full-time employment. For various personal reasons the decision *had* to be made.

At first I was filled with frustration and resentment – frustration with the thought of possibly becoming a "cabbage" after so many years of brain activity, and resentment with the thought of someone else doing my job.

During those forty-two years my life had been filled to the brim. At work I had job satisfaction and loyalties to an employer, and the comradeship and team spirit of my fellow employees. At home I gave my love and attention to a very dear husband and son, my parents whom we looked after in health and sickness until they died, and my brother who was unfortunately divorced and came to us for a home. During my spare(!) time my husband and I visited geriatric wards and elderly people who lived on their own and invited and entertained them in our own home. I personally thrived on it and found it kept me alive and young both in mind and body. At the same time it was all a challenge which I found gave me great fulfilment. I was happy in the knowledge of being *needed* both at work and at home. Hence my fears of retirement.

Once the decision had been made we had to look farther afield for cheaper property in view of the fact we were giving up two incomes at the same time. Then came the trauma of buying and selling houses.

It has taken me three months to unwind and supposedly slow down. Away from the hustle and bustle of town life I have had to *learn* that life

---

Cont.

is *so* different. I am learning to be aware and to appreciate small things I never had time for before, such as feeding the birds who come regularly every morning, watching for the postman and milkman who are so very much on time, and seeing the children mount the school bus each morning. Such small things and yet they are all part and parcel of life. I have learnt that unless you slow down you do not become a whole person.

My fears of *not* being needed have proved wrong. We try to give our love, attention and companionship to the elderly and they truly do appreciate it. The freedom is marvellous and at the same time we have charge of our own lives. Maybe it's a little selfishness – something I haven't had the chance to experience before – but I must admit I am enjoying it to the full.'

This is YOUR life. That has to be one of the meanings of self-realisation. You are now free to be yourself. One of the features of materialist society is that many different goals can all, apparently, be reduced to money or possessions. Inevitably, then, we all get caught up in the same race – a sort of universal fashion prevails throughout the second age of life. An economist, Fred Hirsch, described what happens under pervasive materialism. We end up, he suggests, not by working for what we *need* but for what we *want*, things which in some way set us up alongside the Jones's, or maybe even above them, things which he called 'positional goods' because they give you a position in society. In terms of our list of needs you are now using money not to buy safety or physical survival but the esteem of your neighbours. A bigger hi-fi set, it used to be, now it's a video-recorder or an electronic organ. Do we *need* them or only *want* them? The trouble with that sort of materialism is that it produces a society fuelled by envy, and, inevitably, it is the envy of the many (who are less successful) for the few (who are more successful). It doesn't matter if all get richer because the many still envy the few. For most people it has to be a no-win situation, for no matter how well they do there always seem to be other people doing better. What a relief then to jump off that escalator and find a way of measuring yourself which applies to you alone, so that other people's needs and achievements do not affect it.

Maslow argued that it was a sign of maturity to rise above all the other needs, to jump off the escalator. Hirsch believed in that also, but pointed out that if too many people jumped off there would be no fuel for economic growth in our society. Perhaps he need not have worried. If the second age of life is ruled by materialism there should be enough fuel around to keep the economy moving, leaving those in the third age free to decide to make their own individual scales of happiness and success.

That is the secret of the real freedom of the third age, although some will find it sooner. The rules are no longer set by others so that only a few can win. We have, each of us, to find our own game and make our own rules. Freedom does not mean relaxing.

If you want to pin-point your aspirations a bit more try putting marks of 1 (very little) to 5 (a great deal) against the following 12 possible goals in life. Then see in what order they come out. In another column put the ratings you would have given each twenty years ago. Have things changed?

1 *Leadership.* To become an influential leader; to organise and control others to achieve community or organisational goals.

2 *Expertness.* To become an authority on a special subject; to persevere to reach a hoped-for expert level of skill and accomplishment.

3 *Prestige.* To become well-known, to obtain recognition, awards, or high social status.

4 *Service.* To contribute to the satisfaction of others; to be helpful to others who need it.

5 *Wealth.* To earn a great deal of money; to build up a large financial estate.

6 *Independence.* To have the opportunity for freedom of thought and action; to be one's own boss.

7 *Affection.* To obtain and share companionship and affection through immediate family and friends.

8 *Security.* To achieve a secure and stable position in work and financial situations.

9 *Self-realisation/self-growth.* To optimise personal development; to realise one's full creative and innovative potential; to have a sense of achievement.

10 *Spirituality.* To dedicate oneself totally to the pursuit of ultimate values, ideals, and principles.

11 *Pleasure.* To enjoy life; to be happy and content; to have the good things in life.

12 *Adventure.* To have opportunities for exploration; risks; excitement.

WHAT NEXT?

If you have faithfully followed through the exercises thus far you should have a clearer idea of who you are, where you are in life, and how you got there. May be you are one of the fortunate ones who already know that. It remains to answer the question 'Where do I go from here?' No-one except ourselves can answer that question, of course, although many of us have wished that someone would. Earlier in life there were perhaps too many people, in the parent, teacher, boss rôles, who knew exactly where we should be heading. In one's fifties one stands alone, responsible for oneself. The ideas which follow can only be hints towards creating a self-fulfilling prophecy for yourself. If you know what you want you will certainly improve the odds on getting it.

The last part of that life-line, if you drew it, can provide the first clue. Is it going up or down? Is it firm or weak, short or long? The next step is to try dreaming a little.

Imagine that you are lying in bed, drifting peacefully towards death at a ripe old age. You have just got the strength to write a last letter to your favourite grandchild or an old friend, looking back on your life and on what parts of it you most treasure. The letter will be something for them to remember you by, so it should be all about you, and at this stage you have nothing to lose by telling it all. What would you say in that letter? You would tell what you did and achieved in that important age of working, of course, but you would have to go on to talk about the twenty or thirty years of the third age and of your pleasures and achievements then.

If you can imagine a little of what you might write in that letter about the meaning of life as you found it, then you will have some clues to the goals you will be setting up for yourself for the years to come.

It is not an easy thing to do, to imagine writing that letter. Those who have taken the time to do it, even to write it out, have found that it helps because it lifts them away from the immediate problems and pressures and sets them down at the end of life when such pressures no longer matter. Many of the letters end up by talking about spiritual matters or religion. Not necessarily the church-going part of religion, but the aspects of religion that help one to answer the questions 'What am I for in this vast and changing universe?' and 'What is the meaning of my life?' They are questions which we can duck when we are busy but they do not go away.

If the idea of a letter to your grandchild does not appeal, try to imagine an ideal week. Allow no problems about money, or climate, or health to interfere. Close your eyes and picture where you would be, who you would be with and what you would be doing. If at first you picture the beach of an expensive resort ask yourself how many weeks a year you would like to spend like that and, if it's only a few, think of an alternative ideal week because even the best of holidays pall after a time. They are intended to be escapes from reality and your dream week should be one you would like to repeat again and again. When you have your dream firmly in your mind try to analyse what it is about the week that makes it so ideal. If you can pin that down you may have some clue to your own idea of happiness. If you don't like dreaming about the future, pick instead on a special week in the past and use that, in the same way, to find out what made it special for you.

You may, however, need no dreams to help you define what you want. You know it well enough. The problem is to achieve it. How on earth do you find the peace and seclusion of a country village cottage if you are tied down to a nine-to-five job for the next ten years, living in a high-rise block with no savings and elderly parents to support. Dreams can then be only an impatience, a frustration, and a reminder of what might have been. Life is a prison, and dreaming of the outside can only hurt.

We are all prisoners to some degree, of course, but we do not have to accept a prisoner's philosophy of helplessness. Everyone has some elbow-room, some room for improving the situation. Certainly there will be some constraints that are beyond change – if we are physically handicapped or seriously ill, for instance. But history is full of inspiring examples or people who rose above even these constraints. More often than not the enemy is ourself, our attitudes and disposition. We can choose to let others determine our fate or we can take a hand ourselves.

Audrey Collin of Leicester Polytechnic has developed a diagram to demonstrate the different attitudes that people have to managing their life. Do they see life as open and offering them opportunities or as closed and constraining? Do they actively try to work upon the world about them or passively respond to what turns up? Do they take a long-term or a short-term view? In other words, do they plan years ahead or only for next week? Compressing these questions into two dimensions the diagram looks like this:

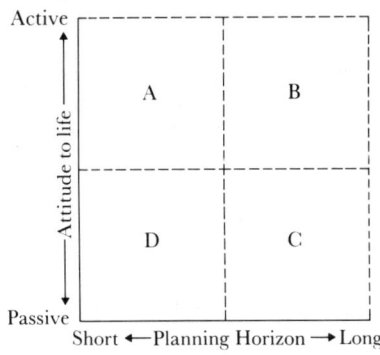

The real floaters are the people in Box D who do not think beyond tomorrow and who feel they have no influence on their own destiny. Such people can be very happy-go-lucky or very depressed, for 'take no thought for tomorrow' is not always a recipe for happiness. Those who fit in Box A are more opportunist – they do not plan, but they do feel able to make the most of whatever situation crops up. Relaxed or rogues, they are seldom depressed because they see life as a bundle of opportunities. People in Box C can get very depressed indeed, as they see life stretching out in a fixed scenario ahead of them. Set up for life by birth and education (or lack of it) as they see it, life can seem like an endless obstacle race which they have no chance of winning. It requires an act of great determination for them to move into Box B where people believe that if you take a long enough view you can affect your own destiny.

The boxes are self-fulfilling prophecies. If you see yourself as life's prisoner you will be. If you really believe that you can influence events you will often be able to. The middle-classes in England have traditionally taken a Box B view, investing in their own and their children's long-term future. British business, some would say, has been either A or at best C in its orientation with too little of the determination and self-confidence of B.

Where are you? There are no rights and wrongs about the boxes, but some consequences. This book will appeal most to those who have an active outlook. Others will see it as describing a few more of the obstacles on life's course, interesting, perhaps, but just more things to worry about.

Can you change your box? Yes, if you want to. But it does require effort and willpower and some idea of how to go about it. Chapter 7 provides some practical ideas about changing for those who are serious about it. The first step, as always, is to decide which box you would like to move to, the start of a self-fulfilling prophecy again.

The fact that change is all around you does not mean that you, the essential you, has to change. We are who we are, and after fifty years we should be getting used to ourselves. It helps, however, to understand what is happening to you and why, even if you decide to do nothing about it. The man with a pain in his stomach was greatly relieved to learn that it was not an ulcer but only indigestion. The pain was still there but he could stop worrying about it.

This book is about understanding what is going on. It is about change but it is not a commandment to change. Changing ourselves is only one of the options. To relax and enjoy it may be another. We remain free to change or not to change, or to change at the fringes but not in essentials. The important thing is that it is *we* who decide.

CHAPTER FIVE

ETWORKS

Only the hermit manages without people to whom he can relate, and even the hermit tries to make sure that he is visited occasionally, or is at least recognised, as the neighbourhood oddity. Most of the rest of us have work, a family, or friends, to provide us with our social networks, the structures for mattering which are crucial to our identity. Because of the changes that are likely to occur in the eighties to those of us in our fifties, we are bound to see some shifts in these networks and structures. Indeed the loss or disruption of a key network may be the one thing in all the changes which really disturbs us. The subject is sufficiently important to need a chapter to itself.

Work I have already discussed. Many people will be changing their patterns of work and leisure as they draw nearer to their sixties. The changes are going to affect how they live, maybe even where they live, as well as the people they meet and the expectations that these people have of them. One year ago I left my full-time job. I did not then fully realise what it would be like not having an office to go to every day, with its routine, its daily gossip, and the endless cups of coffee as well as a desk with my name on it – a visible proof that I mattered. Working from home has many advantages, including all the time saved in *not* gossiping or travelling in overcrowded trains, but it is different. One doesn't matter in such an obvious way. If the telephone is silent and there are no letters or visitors I can feel a forgotten prisoner.

The next thing I realised, as a self-employed person, was that I had to create my own work networks. In a formal job you are locked into work groups, committees, and relationships with other parts of the organisation. Because you are in the accounts department you are automatically in other people's networks. A self-employed person is in no-one's network. Time has to be invested in creating new networks. The restaurants and pubs of our cities are full, at lunch time, of people building networks. Agents, brokers, co-operatives, conferences, associations and clubs are all network-building devices. They will grow in popularity in the eighties as more and more of us have to build our own work networks.

Using redundancy or early retirement as a springboard to doing your own thing sounds splendid, but the ninety-two-per cent of Britain's workers who work in organisations don't work there by accident. We are not loners or hermits by nature, and the new wave of self-employment may put new strains on our social networks, particularly the family section of them.

Work, or the lack of it, is hitting the family network in another way. What do you say to your children when, with all the right O levels and A levels and even, perhaps, degrees, they cannot get a job? How do you justify to them a society which you, at least in their eyes, helped to create? How do you answer their depressed questioning about the point of life? For the wife, instead of a home free at last of noisy teenagers she may still find herself required to provide a hotel for her sons and daughters and their unemployed friends. Having worked and sometimes slaved to help your children aspire to a better life than yours, they are now, through no fault of their own, locked up in your smoke-filled, rock-musicked living room. Where then is their structure for mattering? What then is the responsibility of the family? When, under these conditions, should the individual stand on his or her own?

Our stage in life, even without the problems of the 1980s, would bring its own tensions to traditional structures like the family. The emptying nest, as the children leave home, may be postponed for the reasons given above; alternatively, it can come earlier than it used to now that young people set up establishments of their own before marriage. The simple fact that we have fewer children means that the youngest child grows up earlier in the marriage than in the past with the result that the nest is empty earlier in that marriage. An emptying nest means a change in the way of life of both parents who now have more time and fewer people in the family structure. It is not a new dilemma but it still comes as a new one to each couple.

But the world of the eighties is different from the world of the fifties or sixties when most of us got married. One in four of *our* generation is likely to have divorced and remarried. That complicates the structure, bringing in step-children, ex-wives and ex-husbands. The family, as I suggested in Chapter 1, often has a different shape today. Grandparents live long enough to be great-grandparents and parents multiply so that the family is top-heavy, as it were – an inverted pyramid, with the parents in the middle, trying or not trying to hold it together. Given a rapidly changing society it is inevitable that there will be many different values, standards, and concepts of morality within the pyramid. Sex is only the most obvious example. The view of sex as a private and almost secret matter, linked with the obvious possibilities of sex as sin, which conditioned the childhood and adolescence of most of us, has given way to a concept of sex as leisure, if not sex as sport in some circles. It is not easy to live with people who have different views on such vital issues. Nor are our fifties going to be immune to changing values. If sex is now a competitive sport what does this mean for the marriage? How do people in structures like a family sort these things out?

I cannot in this chapter provide nice neat answers to these questions. What I can do is to provide some conceptual frameworks which may offer clues to what is going on. I can outline my own answers, and the ways I search for them but I can only hope that they will encourage you to work out your own. Shifts in networks, such as work or the family, are inevitable. They can also be a way of moving us onward to another scene, another act. But there is no denying that they are inconvenient, even painful, at the time.

A wife, who kept her job as a lecturer after her husband lost his in advertising, describes how it affected their marriage. Her husband now earns his living from his business consultancy – just. She pays their mortgage and, as his official partner, is liable for his debts.

'That's fine,' she points out, 'as long as you stay married. But although I take my own career seriously, I do basically believe that the man should support the family. That feeling – which I can't justify – is behind what has driven us apart, and we would divorce now except that the financial ties are too tight to face. He found it difficult to come to me for money at the start, and I understood that. But it was a little later, when I began to think that he should be on his feet by now, that the trouble started.

I'd make absurd gestures – like buying cheap joints which I never had the time to cook for long enough, so they were inedible. I'd dare him to grumble and then make some subtle remark which means "Well, if you weren't such a failure, we could eat better food".

There's nothing I can say to defend how I behave, but however hard I try, I feel that if he cannot support me, I would be better not holding him up. Now that his business has picked up, there's nothing left between us to salvage, so we would probably both be better looking after our own separate interests. It's funny, there's never been another man or another woman – we just couldn't adjust and forget the brainwashing about expectations to make our relationship grow or change once he lost his job. That job was the cement of our marriage, a necessary part for both of us of the way we saw each other.'

For women like her, the Protestant work ethic has created an expectation of a husband who will climb steadily up the branches of the company tree, until he arrives at virtuous retirement at the age of 65. With that go the private schools, the cavity-free children's teeth, the foreign holidays, and the mortgage. It adds up to a complete life style.

The Guardian, 29 September 1981

THE WEB OF LIFE

The first step to a conceptual framework is to get some definition of the various structures in one's own life. Imagine life as a web of connections with other people. Put yourself at the middle of it and then, literally, draw the lines that connect you to all the other people in your life. If they are close and special to you, put them close. If they aren't that important draw them far away. Join those together which belong together, the people in an office, or your in-laws, for instance. The drawing will begin to look something like this.

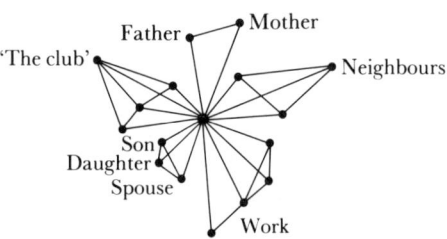

You will be surprised to find how many lines you need to draw. Few people in their fifties will get away with less than thirty if they really pause to think about it. This web of relationships is your 'social network'.

Each of those separate relationships is a blend of loves, fears, worries, and hopes. You have a view of each person at the end of one of these lines, as well as an expectation of what they will do for you or with you. We know how we expect them to react to us, how they will or should behave in certain situations and what will be impossible or unfair to ask of them. We know, roughly, what we want from them and what they want from us. We can compress all of that into the concept of the 'unwritten contract', an unwritten and, usually, unspoken contract that exists between us and every single member of our social networks.

Contracts are about exchanges and expectations. Each party to the contract expects something of the other and, in return, will expect to give something. If they are not spelled out or written down, however, the contracts can mean quite different things to different parties. Since the contracts in social relationships seldom get made explicit we can, some of us, go through life in a continual state of disappointment or disillusion when our expectations remain unfulfilled. It may be, however, that the other party to the contract never knew what was expected of them. This can be particularly true of the small print of social contracts, for contracts have tiny clauses as well as big ones.

In the early days of our marriage I encouraged my wife to pursue her own career. What I never made plain to her, or I think, to myself, was that I expected her to do all the conventional housewifely things as well. 'You don't love me', I remember saying, when there was no evening meal, and the breakfast things still littered the table, when what I meant was 'You haven't kept the bargain which I had in my mind but forgot to tell you about.' One young marriage nearly foundered because the two partners had different expectations as to who cleaned the shoes. In her house it had been the man's job, in his it was do-it-yourself. They didn't talk about it, just growled. It was a tiny clause in an unspoken contract which could have been renegotiated if they had thought of it in that way.

Contracts naturally change over the years; unfortunately we don't always wake up in time to the fact that the old understanding is now out of date and a new contract is needed. For want of a revised contract, the relationship crumbles. Children, for instance, are always complaining that contracts linger on too long, that they are not allowed to grow up. The story of Mary and Elaine, below, is an example of things being the other way round.

The mother–daughter contract

Mary was a reluctant mother. She had never enjoyed the rôle but had done her duty as she saw it, making sure that Elaine grew up with all the right habits and training. When Elaine was able to leave school and survive on her own as a secretary, Mary was much relieved. Now she could go back to her own life and her own interests.

As she grew older Mary counted herself lucky to have a daughter, now married herself with two children, to look after her and help her, particularly after she was widowed and had to learn to live on her own. Unfortunately she found Elaine was bossy rather than helpful, always ordering her about and complaining about her inadequacies.

Elaine in turn resented her mother's dependence on her. She felt that Mary had never been a proper mother, had never provided that haven of security and peace which motherhood and home should be. Even now, in her fifties, she still hoped Mary could be a true mother to her and comfort her in her many little problems and troubles. Instead of that she found that she was now supposed to be a mother to Mary, she who had never had a proper mother herself. It wasn't fair.

They were truly fond of each other, Mary and Elaine, but any meeting between them was bound to produce friction. They were working on different contracts.

Thirty contracts in one social network are a lot to consider. Most of them will have worked themselves out over time so that there is an understood code of behaviour. Our social networks eventually become quite comfortable as we work out the contracts by trial and error. And then it changes. Key members of the network move away (the children perhaps). Someone dies. You change your job and a whole chunk of the network has to be replaced. You move house, and new neighbours come into focus while old ones fade away. Your rôle changes at work because you are promoted. That part of the network stays the same, the people don't change, but the contracts do. Your old colleagues are now your subordinates. Sad though it is, things can't be *quite* the same again. Many a person has determined that their promotion will make no difference to their relationship with their old colleagues but it always does. It has to, because the rôles are different and so will be your colleagues' expectations of you. Adolescence is known to be the time for re-working contracts with parents and other adults; it is a particularly tough time because, usually, all the contracts need to be re-worked at the same time. Leaving school means new friends, new superiors, just at the time when parents should be letting go. There is no stable part in the whole arrangement. Adults are more lucky, because usually it is only one bit of the network that changes at any one time. But the fifties can be one time when there are almost as many changes as in adolescence. By then, however, we *should* be better able to cope.

CHANGING CONTRACTS

Important changes in one's place in the network are often marked by public ceremonies or rituals. These are important because they are signs to the world around you that your rôle has changed and that all contracts are now up for revision. Marriage is one obvious change which is surrounded by a lot of ritual, or used to be. The father 'gives away' his daughter, a public sign that she is no longer his responsibility. The bride and groom actually make a new contract in front of witnesses, be it in Church or the Register Office. There are ritual speeches, ritual humour, and much merry-making. The networks of both partners are invited to be there so that all concerned may know that a change in contracts has occurred.

There are some signs that the marriage ritual is becoming less public, less important. More people have small unfussy weddings. Some do not bother at all. This may mean that marriage, in some social settings, is no longer the dramatic change in contracts that it used to be. People leave homes and parents long before marriage, they work together and increasingly live together without requiring people to look at them differently or treat them differently. Women may choose not to change their surname on marriage. A wedding then is more a private exchange of promises rather than a public announcement to the world, which does not need to know.

86

Puberty used to be an important staging post in life, celebrated by confirmation, or its equivalent in different religions, in which the young person publicly takes responsibility for his or her life. People are expected to treat him or her differently from then on. The independence of children from an early age has as much to do with the disappearance of puberty rites as does the decline of religious belief. The public ritual is no longer necessary because puberty in itself does not mean a change in contract.

Death has its own set of rituals. These are very important to the bereaved, partly because of the structure and support they bring to life in the difficult days that follow a death, but partly because they announce to all we know that things are different now. 'She has died. I am a widower.' 'My father is dead. I am now the responsible adult in the family.'

There are, however, new change points in life for which new rituals have not yet emerged. Retirement, redundancy, and divorce, all require major changes in one's networks and contracts, yet convention suggests that we keep as quiet as possible about these events. Retirement often has some small rituals within the firm or the office – a party, a speech, a clock to mark the hours that we now have to learn to fill; but they are ending rituals not starting rituals. They announce to the network which we are leaving that we are going. Sadly, there is nothing to announce to the world beyond the office that we have arrived.

Divorce parties have been known. Some find them tasteless but, again, they do have the function of announcing a change. We could do with more parties for redundancy, for the children leaving home, or for moving house to a new neighbourhood. In a secular society we cannot call on religion to do it for us; we will have to invent our own methods. Here it is tempting to call on the fifties generation to start setting a few new fashions because without these outward and visible signs it is harder to make a public re-structuring of our life.

Ritual as a calendar

Rituals have traditionally been used to measure the passing of seasons. Harvest, winter, spring, and summer, all had their festivals, celebrated in different ways in different lands. The rituals not only provide an excuse for a holiday, they also mark the staging points in the year, reminding us to concentrate on new activities and helping to relieve the monotony of the daily grind.

It is sad that the industrial age has found so few equivalents of its own to match those that were so fitting in the agricultural world. More small firms are now experimenting with closing their whole operation twice or thrice a year for everyone to have a simultaneous holiday, as

---

Cont.

used to happen in Wakes week in the textile industry. It was an opportunity for the simultaneous celebration of the work that was central to the lives of all the families.

Or should the annual company meeting be a festival occasion? In some Cathedral Closes there is still an Audit Party to celebrate the annual closing of the books of account.

The seasons of a man's year need to be marked just as much as the seasons of his life. Work without ritual is monotony.

THE FAMILY WHEN WE ARE FIFTY

The informal contracts in marriage and families need continual revision, but do not always get it. Families change all the time. At present one in four contracts are broken irretrievably (by divorce), but it may be that some earlier revision of those contracts would have made the final break unnecessary. Even the three-quarters of all marriages which survive will require the unwritten contracts to change over time. Those couples who can, explicitly or implicitly, adapt their marriage and family patterns over the years are most likely to find that marriage is a springboard for life, not a trap. Changes inside the marriage can make outside changes unnecessary.

Some research which Pam Berger and I did into the marriage patterns of business executives ten years ago investigated the changes which might be needed to keep the marriage alive. The research looked at what the individuals in twenty-three marriages wanted out of life and how those needs and ambitions helped to determine the way they arranged their lives together. The suggestion that follows from the research is that as our priorities change in life, so too must the arrangement of our lives, particularly of our marriages since marriage is for most people one of the key structures for mattering, a vital part of their social network.

The individuals all answered a questionnaire which produced scores for them on sixteen different kinds of priorities. The four priorities which were most crucial turned out to be:

Dominance　or the desire to have power and influence over others
Achievement　or the desire to succeed in something, not necessarily business (these two were linked together quite closely)
Nurturance　or the desire to look after people
Autonomy　or the desire to do your own thing (these two were opposites, if you scored high on one you scored low on the other)

The individuals were then plotted on to a chart according to their scores on these four priorities:

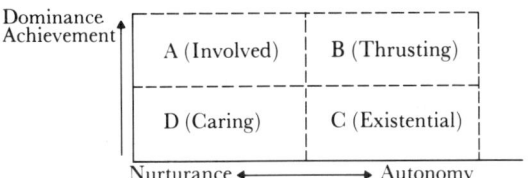

```
Dominance
Achievement ↑  ┌ ─ ─ ─ ─ ─ ─ ┬ ─ ─ ─ ─ ─ ─ ┐
               │             ┊             │
               │ A (Involved)┊ B (Thrusting)│
               │             ┊             │
               ├ ─ ─ ─ ─ ─ ─ ┼ ─ ─ ─ ─ ─ ─ ┤
               │             ┊             │
               │ D (Caring)  ┊ C (Existential)│
               │             ┊             │
               └ ─ ─ ─ ─ ─ ─ ┴ ─ ─ ─ ─ ─ ─ ┘
          Nurturance ←─────────→ Autonomy
```

In this particular group of young business executives it turned out that half the men were thrusters, in Box B, but there was one B woman, who was herself an executive as well as a wife. Half of the women were caring, in Box D. The more successful men, in financial terms only, were, as you might expect, the ones in Box B.

That was quite interesting, but more interesting were the different life styles and marriage patterns that emerged when the individuals in each marriage were paired up on the chart.

The most common marriage was a B–D one, a Thrusting husband married to a Caring wife. They had a truly traditional marriage pattern. The husband earned the money, the wife managed the home and the children. Where his work led him she followed. He had his friends, she had hers, and the only joint friends were family. He had his leisure interests, golf or football or squash; she had hers, usually during weekdays. She did the housekeeping, he looked after the booze. The houses were traditionally arranged, with a sitting room, a dining room (if there were enough rooms) and kitchen. The children were well-disciplined and, at this age of six to ten, had their own evening meal separately from their parents. When the parents did have their meal or talked together they preferred to talk about things or events ('What I did today'. 'Are we going to the pictures tomorrow?', 'Is your mother coming to stay?'), rather than issues or ideas in areas like politics or religion or world affairs. They had steady marriages and if they had an individual problem they felt they should keep it to themselves, rather than load it on to the other. He would take the dog for a walk, if he was stressed, or bang the golfball into the distance. She would lie down alone in her bedroom. The contracts in these marriages were clear and different for husband and wife. As far as I could tell they had never spoken about these contracts. They inherited their view of their respective rôles from their past and adopted them without question.

That life-style was quite different from the next most common pattern, the A–A one, in which both partners come from the A group. Both partners had had full-time jobs when they married and the wife still worked but usually only part-time because she, like all the group, had young children.

Being in the same quarter of our chart means that they had the same priorities, a blend of ambition and the need to look after people.

They were, in other words, marriages of like-minded people. We called them 'involved'.

In these marriages nothing was as tidily arranged as in the B–D traditional marriage. Although at the time of the research the husband was the main earner in the family it wasn't necessarily so, the wife feeling that she carried part of the financial responsibility. Housework was not a high priority, but whoever felt that it needed doing did it, while weekend meals were as often as not prepared by the husband. Their friends were all common friends; except for the people they both met at work they had no separate friends. Their children were either 'advanced' or 'undisciplined' according to your viewpoint and they certainly played a full, almost adult part in the house, sharing in all the meals and conversations. These conversations would as often as not be arguments or discussions about politics or sex or religion rather than about the practical details of their lives. The house itself reflected this mingling of rôles. All the rooms had a more or less common purpose; they were living-rooms rather than bed, sitting, or cooking, rooms and a general air of informality infused the home. If these couples had problems, because they were both high on the caring dimension they shared them. This often meant late nights of talking followed by long days at the office. These couples sometimes seemed to be running to keep up with life, but life was full and, often enough, enjoyable. These couples did explicitly talk with each other about their different rôles and what they wanted from life and from each other. The 'contract' would not have been an alien idea in these marriages.

There was one B–B marriage between two very competitive people (Thrusters) with no children. It was another marriage of similar people but very different from the previous ones. They argued and competed with each other about work and home, but it was competitive not aggressive behaviour. With two full incomes and no children they lived richly, with a lot of 'going out' to entertainment. They used each other as a foil, but seemed to thrive on it. The contract here was very much an instinctive unspoken one.

There were also two C–C marriages, the pairing of two loners. Their pattern of marriage emphasised the importance to them of independence. In one house there were no armchairs, no common table to eat from. The family did not eat or sit together but lived in their own bed-sitting rooms, cooking their own meals and managing their own schedules. Husband and wife were both very busy at their own work and had actually to book meetings with each other to discuss any practical problems of housekeeping or the care of their children. It was a household of equals, but without any obvious expression of community. These C–C marriages can be very stable, because neither partner has very high expectations of it. They are 'marriages of convenience' and as such can be very convenient to both partners, allowing them to pursue their own careers and interests. In these marriages the practical details of the contract had to be discussed even if the more intangible things were passed over.

These were the patterns emerging from this group of young executives, middle-class and in their thirties. Other groups of other ages and in other circumstances have recognised the patterns but have suggested that life is not stable. The pattern of marriage which suits at one stage of life will cause problems later on. The patterns, and the implied contracts which lie behind them have to change. The A–A marriage of involved equals is very often the style appropriate to the first years of marriage. Then it may be that the couple have children – someone has to tend them, and in our society that is still more often than not the rôle of the wife. At the same time the husband's job becomes important, partly because more money is now needed. The pattern moves towards the traditional B–D marriage. This may, however, be only a temporary phase and indeed the recent census suggested that only five per cent of British households completely fitted this pattern on that census date in 1980.

When the children become more independent the marriage can move back into an A–A pattern of involved equals, although in many cases it seems to move to the C–C pattern, the marriage of two loners. One man, who complained constantly about his marriage, was eventually asked by his bored colleague why he stayed married if it was so unpleasant. He thought for a while, then, 'Because of the laundry, I suppose,' he said. It must by then have been a C–C marriage.

Many couples claim that they change patterns all the time. During the week it might be a traditional B–D marriage but it turns into an A–A situation at the weekend and even into a D–B pattern in the holidays with the husband taking over the D or supportive rôle.

What about the fifties? It is often a time of major pattern change. Release from the responsibilities of the children (on average the last child is married when the parents are in their late forties or early fifties) can free the wife to move out of the D box, with its emphasis on caring. But she may not want to. That situation then becomes 'the empty nest syndrome', a wife who misses the responsibilities which kept her in the D box, and finds that she no longer has a full rôle in life. On the other hand, she may find that the responsibilities of looking after children are now replaced by the need to care for ageing parents. The great majority of people over seventy-five do not live in institutions. They live by themselves or with their relatives. In either case the first responsibility for tending them falls upon the children but the children are now in their fifties. It is only when they refuse to accept this responsibility, or cannot cope with it, that the professional caring services take over. For more and more women in their fifties the D box, the caring rôle, will be a trap from which they cannot escape. The empty nest problem may become the never-empty nest problem.

The Empty Nest – Does it matter?

I can't tell you what a relief it was to find myself with an empty nest. Oh, when the last child left . . . for a day or so there was a kind of throb, but, believe me, it was only a day or two.'

Or

'If it's hard now, it's because I don't know what I'll be doing, not because the children are gone. Their going is a blessing; it's time. But I'm scared.'

Or

'I mean, I really love them. You know, I gave them my life for all these years. And I miss them, too, I really do.'

Or— Is it the father's problem?

'For me it's enough! They've been here long enough – maybe too long. It's a funny thing though. All these years Fred was too busy to have much time for the kids, now he's the one who's depressed because they're leaving. He's really having trouble letting go. He wants to gather them around and keep them right here in this house.'

Women speaking to Lillian Rubin, from Lillian B. Rubin's *Women of a Certain Age*.

On the other hand, for some, there may be even more dramatic re-arrangements. If job-work does begin to disappear for people in their middle-to-late fifties the husband may be at home rather more. Part-time work, after a period of cut-back in the early 1980s, will begin to increase again, particularly for women. The man may find himself cast, unwillingly or reluctantly, into the caring rôle – the D box – as a house-husband, while the wife picks up more of the breadwinner rôle. That D–B marriage will mean a major revision of the contracts. In our fifties we have come to terms with our dreams and expectations and face up to the reality of what we have achieved and become. This often results in a re-balancing of home and work, and a reassessment of what the marriage means.

All this has been written as if the family has been a constant unit. For many, of course, this is not true. Divorce is less common in one's fifties than at earlier ages, but nearly twenty per cent of the people now in their fifties will have been divorced at some stage. Divorce quite inevitably complicates the contracts, mainly because there have to be more of them, but partly because it is much less clear what is expected of each person – the possible contracts are almost endless.

Changing contracts in marriage

A wife speaking. 'It changed a lot in the last six years. Earlier on it was terrible! He was the husband who comes home from his work and who picks up his newspaper at the same time as he switches on the television. We had a talkative little boy who he totally ignored. And me – everything, but everything, fell on my shoulders. He was physically there, but that's all.'

'What led to the change over the last years?'

'Well, we had some very violent arguments. We had long, long discussions which at times didn't seem to get anywhere. We forgot all about it! And slowly things seemed to get better.

I'm still not satisfied but he's more attentive than he was before.'

A husband speaking. 'I suppose like everybody else I've always wanted to be the Company president. But the price that one has to pay is too high. I've seen these guys up on the sixth floor, and the stress that they are under. God help them – I certainly don't envy them any longer. So I made a decision a few years back to pay more attention to my family, and I don't regret it. I suppose you could say that I've matured, become more realistic about my chances, if you like.'

A wife speaking. 'I worry about the future, because I think I'm going to need them more than they need me. Because I've consciously given up a lot of my career time for them. Perhaps I expect more of them than I should? I don't know whether that makes sense or not. I sort of expect them to be fulfilling! I say to them, "You know, you've got to be fulfilling." I'm very ambivalent about it really. In one way I resent the time they take up, in another way John (the eldest) is growing away from me. That's the way it should be, but I think it's a bit sad.'

Reported in P. Evans and F. Bartolome, *Must Success Cost So Much.*

The modern family of two divorced and remarried parents, each perhaps with a previous family of their own, gives new meaning to the extended family. The extended family used to mean the clutter of aunts, uncles, and cousins that resulted when there were five or more children in any family. Now it is the nuclear family, the core family, which is extending in unusual ways. It is extending upwards, as more people live to a ripe old age, so that many young children today know their great-grandparents. Fifty years ago they would only have known half their grandparents, the others being dead. It is also extending outwards to include half-brothers and sisters, step-fathers and step-mothers and those for whom there is as yet no collective name, the children brought into the family by the new step-parent, children with no blood connection with their new semi-brother and sisters. So comparatively recent is this new sort of extended family that we know very little about it. Anecdote suggests that it *can* be very enriching and stimulating family *if* the contracts are understood in the same way for everyone. It can also go horribly wrong – but so can more ordinary families.

Marriage contracts

'I view our marriage as very happy. We are both busy people but we try always to find time at the end of the day to talk things over, to share our worries and hopes and fears. That's the best part of being married – having someone to share things with. The children are almost grown up now and it's exciting watching them and, occasionally, joining them. Of course there are rows, but we try to talk them through even if it means long nights arguing. Then we have lots of friends and are quite busy locally in the community. Life sometimes feels too full, but it's fun.'

An A–A marriage

'I would say that we are both quite successful in our own fields. Luckily they overlap, so we can discuss each other's problems. We argue a great deal. She is my fiercest critic and I hers. Sometimes the arguments get quite stormy. We decided long ago not to have children. Sometimes I regret that but it would have meant Sheila giving up her ambitions and she was not going to do that – she's very talented. Life is exciting rather than comfortable, but I don't think I could stand being married to some home-maker. I would get so bored.'

A B–B marriage

'We are very companionable. It has been a good partnership. He has done very well in his job and is still lucky enough to have one, we have a nice house and can be pleased with the way the children have worked out. Sometimes I think our life has been a bit boring but you can't have everything, can you? We have a lot to be thankful for.'

A B–D marriage

'We go our different ways. He has his world and I have mine. Oh, we get on alright and we talk about practical things like finance and repairs and cars, but I wouldn't say we were intimate. It's a convenience, our marriage, not a fantastic experience, but I like it that way. It lets me be free.'

A C–C marriage

Our fifties are bound to be a time for family contract reviewing. It is as well to face up to it and do it as consciously as you can. Realise at least that it is happening. For most people all the rôles in the family are now different. The children are now adults, but the parents are a new responsibility. The work-rôles of husband and wife may be changing. All these changes will be reflected in a different set of priorities for each person. On the marriage diagram each person will move to a different box, demanding a different relationship with those closer to them. Check your contracts before you settle down again.

The facts about the elderly

There are about three million people over seventy-five in Britain today. In ten years time there will be an extra half a million.

About six per cent of these are looked after in hospitals or old people's homes. Another ten per cent need some form of regular care and tending. Most of the rest live either with a spouse, or with children. In 1971 half of all elderly people who were severely handicapped lived with their children. Only five per cent of elderly people (over seventy-five) live alone.

It has been estimated that a typical man and wife, married in 1920 and now in their eighties, would have forty-two surviving female relatives, fourteen of whom would not be at work.

A couple who married in 1950 and will be in their eighties in the early years of the next century will by then only have eleven surviving female relatives, three of whom would not be at work.

Will there be enough 'family' to go round?

Reported by Roy Parker in 'Tending and Social Policy', in *A New Look at the Personal Social Services*, PSI Discussion Paper, February 1981

ARRANGING THE NETWORK

Families are only one chunk of the social network in which we live. In fact, for a few they may be a very small chunk, even non-existent. They may all have died, or faded away, or we may have turned our back on them at some time. The full social network has many groups besides the family groups, which we need to think about as we get older.

There are three views, or theories, about the way people behave as they grow older. One says that people increasingly 'disengage' from relationships, life becoming increasingly quiet and solitary. Another view holds that people want to stay 'alive' as long as they can. Eventually it is poor health or lack of opportunity to participate in society which forces them to disengage. A third view stresses the 'continuity' in all our lives, maintaining that the present is only the prelude to the future, we are who we are and we change as little as we can.

There are good examples of all these views. We all know people who increasingly drop out of life, seemingly quite happy to meditate or doze through their third age, 'rocking-chair people' one research study called them; but we also know people still vigorous and active in their nineties and today in Britain there are over two thousand people beyond one hundred, many of them still active. Others continue as they were, 'the same only slower'. The truth has to be a mix of all these.

That is good news. It means that we have choice. Nothing is fixed except that we will grow increasingly older. All the studies, however, have two things in common – they all make some connection between the individual and his or her surrounding social network (to disengage means, for example, leaving the network), and they all suggest that whatever pattern we finally adopt, it took ten years or so to develop. We do not just decide to disengage and then do it tomorrow – it is a slow and gradual process. Indeed, when it comes suddenly, as in unexpected widowhood, divorce, or redundancy, we go into a state of shock.

Our fifties then, are an excellent time to begin to reorganise the network and re-think the contracts with the different groups before this is forced upon us by change.

The fifties, in other words, are the time to make the investments in yourself and in connections with others which will pay dividends in your sixties and seventies.

Consider, therefore, the different chunks of the network. Which will continue beyond the fifties, which will fade away? The group of work colleagues will change for almost everyone. Only those whose work continues, the same only slower, until the end, like farmers, writers, and some politicians, will see this as a continuing major chunk. For most people, too, the family is a diminishing although still important chunk as they get older. The old parents die, the married children have their own lives. Sisters and brothers are older and probably distant. Grandchildren visit only occasionally. Family becomes less of a mainstay and more of a lifeboat when things go seriously wrong. For some people these two chunks, work and family, make up the whole network during their middle years, that second age of work. Remove them both and you have a forced disengagement. Suddenly the convoy which surrounded you disappears and you are left alone on the sea of life. No wonder that retirement can lead to depression, apathy and even early death.

It is easy, in that second age of life, to over-invest in one or two parts of the network. Time seems short, life busy, work is interesting and demanding, the family is growing, money is short, there is so much to do. Friends are often no more than acquaintances, met at the pub or the party. Hobbies or part-time interests get squeezed out and television or watching football are not activities that require other people – they do not link you into another network. The fifties, therefore, can be a time to start correcting that imbalance while the network is still around you. This is another reason why pocket-money work and gift-work become important – both of them mean that you have to get involved with people. You can collect stamps or old brasses on your own, do carving or pottery or grow beans on your own, but once you start to sell them, or give them away to stalls and charities, you are connected to groups of people. You may take a stall at the Saturday market, or join the finance committee of a local charity, or organise the darts competition in the local pub. You could go into local politics, found a new society to promote the cause you are interested in, or set up a business in the back shed.

There are so many examples of people, stirred perhaps by the death of a child or a husband, who start major schemes to raise money to help those who are similarly afflicted, or of others who turn their passions into business – the gourmet who opens a restaurant, the photographer who becomes the local children's portraitist. All these one can do whilst still connected to one's principal networks. They are, whatever their other merits, ways of investing in future networks.

Building new networks

Bridge

Biography: Female, aged forty-eight, married. Full-time housewife and part-time bridge teacher at local adult education evening institute.
Project: Member of card-playing family but only developed serious interest in bridge after regular games with a friend in need of social contact. Played at local and then national level and, as quality of opposition improved, so experienced consequent refinement of skills. Pleasure of playing a continual reinforcement, especially in her enjoyment of competitive success. Timing of project at an appropriate stage in her life – impossible to have developed a similar commitment in early motherhood. Encouraged her son's interest in bridge as well as that of work colleagues and students. Length of project: fourteen years.

Philately

Biography: Male, aged fifty-two, married. Left school at fourteen and in early adulthood emigrated to Australia. Now living in England and foreman at motor car assembly plant.
Project: Schoolboy interest rekindled after twenty-five year gap whilst working in Australia and seeing stamps on letters other workers received from their home countries. Collecting for its own sake gradually replaced by interest in production of stamps and then participation in club competitions. Knowledge derived initially from magazines but deliberately sought to expand his knowledge through club membership. Such membership provides good sources of contacts and materials and is regarded as necessary to attainment of expert status. Length of project: Twelve years.

Cont.

Ornithology

Biography: Female, aged sixty-two, married. Left grammar school at sixteen and became a commercial designer before opening a sweet-shop. Now a freelance writer.

Project: Interest traced back to farm childhood. Knowledge developed through solitary walking and observation and assembled extensive personal reference library. Participated in national nest record scheme and co-founder of two societies as well as belonging to many others. Began weekly nature column for local paper and has since published two small books herself, contributing to one other. Continually developing new interests, more recently in wildlife photography. Has apprenticed several youngsters in bird recognition by taking them on her walks and compiled a slide show for schools and colleges. Length of project: Thirty years.

From research study of Dr Stephen Brookfield reported in *'Independent Adult Learning'*, Studies in Adult Education. Vol. 13 No. 1, 1981

You do have choice. The formal research on growing older is agreed on at least one thing: the people who *choose* what they want are the happy ones. The ones who feel that it had all descended on them are depressed. The fifties are a time for choice. Don't wait until you can't choose, is one message from all that we know. A second is that all networks need a stable core. It is, as I shall suggest in a later chapter, much easier to change things at the edges. What is the core of our networks? If it is the work-group then there is, in the longer term, a real danger that you will lose your most important structure for mattering when you lose your job. What will you have to fall back on?

Eight out of ten people today live in a family unit headed by a married couple. It is an important fact to remember in an age which appears to celebrate individualism. Does this mean that, in spite of everything, divorce, shifting values, and more independence, the family is still the major structure for mattering for most of us? Will it continue that way?

Relationships depend, I have argued, on getting the contracts right. That process has to start with honesty, and truth and, wherever possible, with love and understanding. It could not be better put than the way John Wood has expressed it in this poem:

Poem for everyman
I will present you
parts
of
my
self
slowly
if you are patient and tender.
I will open drawers
that mostly stay closed
and bring out places and people and things
sounds and smells, loves and frustrations, hopes and sadnesses,
bits and pieces of three decades of life
that have been grabbed off
in chunks
and found lying in my hands.
They have eaten
their way into my memory
carved their way into my
heart
altogether – you or I will never see them –
they are me.
If you regard them lightly
deny that they are important
or worse, judge them
I will quietly, slowly
begin to wrap them up,
in small pieces of velvet,
like worn silver and gold jewelry,
tuck them away
in a small wooden chest of drawers

and close.

John Wood, from *How do you feel?*

CHAPTER SIX

*F*ACING
THE WORRIES

The Age (being fifty) and the Decade (the eighties) have as much danger in them as they have opportunity, to go back to the Chinese diagram at the start of the book. Anyone who is not a little worried must be detached from reality; for change, as I have argued, is inevitable, both in society at large and in our own situations. Change means uncertainty and uncertainty means worry.

There are the cataclysmic worries – war, violence, famine, or revolution. 'The Unthinkables', someone called them, because it is hard to know what to do about them. They are not the subject of this book, but no-one living in the 1980s can dismiss these clouds on the horizon.

Then there are the worries that particularly concern people in their fifties contemplating the third age: 'What shall I do?', 'What shall I be?' 'What opportunities will there be in the society which is emerging?' These are the crucial identity issues of this time in our life and I have tried, in the earlier chapters, to suggest how one might go about answering the questions they raise.

Thirdly, there are the very practical problems of organising one's life, coping with the stress which is all too prevalent today, and the worries about health and money. This chapter is about these very practical worries.

We must, however, keep worry in perspective. What evidence there is of the views of the contemporary middle-aged suggests that they see at least as much opportunity as worry.

John Nicholson interviewed a range of people in their fifties in Essex as part of his research for his book *Seven Ages*, published in 1980.

Forty eight per cent of the men and twenty-eight per cent of the women in their fifties described their health as excellent, compared with thirty-four per cent and seventeen per cent of those in their forties.

Forty per cent of the men and thirty-two per cent of the women described themselves as less sexually active than they were ten years previously but the *majority* of both sexes reported no change.

They complained, however, of being in limbo – not old enough for all the privileges of old age but too old to be young. On the threshold of the third age?

For the middle classes, the fifties seem to be a noticeably easier period to negotiate than for the working classes. The middle classes feel more secure, more philosophical about the future and are happier to capitalise on their experience and to enjoy their memories. Among working-class men and women there was more resentment, more feeling of being threatened and unwanted.

There is no doubt that younger people are impressed by the wisdom of those in their fifties and turn to them for advice in preference to their contemporaries.

Intellectual abilities remain unimpaired in the fifties but it may be more difficult to handle new information at speed. For example, learning to drive a car or to operate a complex new piece of machinery will be more difficult for many than when they were young.

Ten per cent of women report that they are incapacitated by the menopause, but between five and twenty-five per cent report no symptoms at all.

Most of the women had had enough of motherhood by their fifties; as one put it 'I think you tend to live for your children while you are bringing them up, but once they become the age that mine are now, they're off your hands, and you start living for yourself.'

Do women in their fifties feel differently from men? A survey of fifty women between forty-five and fifty-five was undertaken by Beatrice Musgrave and Zoe Menell for their book *Change and Choice, Women and Middle Age*, published in 1980. Half of the women were from England, half of them were working, and most were middle class with sixteen per cent from a working-class background. The authors give many quotations to illustrate the attitudes and feelings of the women they interviewed. They conclude that the problems of the menopause have been greatly exaggerated. More important, for many women, is the uncertainty about their rôle when the children have left home when society provides few outlets in work or in other structures outside the home. The fact that a quarter of married life is now lived together without the children is becoming a problem for some, particularly those contemplating their husband's retirement. Several are questioning their lifelong commitment to one relationship and find themselves envying the freer life-styles of their children. The increase in public consciousness of sex and of individual fulfilment have tended to raise these women's expectations of what they want out of life and relationships. On the other hand, the increasing consciousness has also made many of them aware of their own resources and of the opportunities 'out there' for their newly discovered abilities. Many of them, too, stressed that a stable relationship was the basis for any advance into the future and a significant number saw their middle years as their golden years: 'Time to pick up threads from the past and begin to think ahead; to cultivate personal resources, acquire skills and seek new outlets with a view to the creative use of capacities'.

Helen Frank in her book *Prime Time* (listed in Chapter 9) gives another excellent description of the views and attitudes of women in middle-age. It is clear from these accounts and several others that in many ways women are better equipped than many men for what the 1980s have to offer. Women in their fifties are used to 'flexilives', to a complex, untidy mixture of work and home and leisure or self-development, more accustomed to having to organise themselves, to define themselves in terms other than their work, and to get fulfilment from a variety of sources. Women, too, live longer than men and have always known this, so their friendships tend to be longer-lasting than men whilst at the same time they are more prepared for alone-ness. The contraceptive pill may have come too late for many women now in their fifties but the aura of choice and personal freedom which effective contraception has brought to women has infected them all, raising their sights to a new concept of what self-fulfilment can mean for them.

Women and men in their fifties today face very similar problems. The empty nest and the emptying factory bring the same worries about what to do, how to live, and who to be. Maybe men have a lot to learn from women. Maybe that is already happening, as men discover that there is a touch of the feminine in all of them, that men too can be 'carers' and not only 'thrusters' and that work does not have to provide a man's total identity.

ORGANISING ONE'S LIFE

It is never easy to organise one's life, and it may get more instead of less difficult in the years ahead. This is because the numbers of different but smaller networks will tend to increase once we drop the big network which is our job or our growing family. Self-employed people nearly always lead busier lives than other people, because they have to manage more than one network simultaneously. The many women who combine work and home-management in a flexilife have a more complicated organisation problem than the man who goes off to the same office every day. As we move out of full-time employment into a life with more choice and variety we will also experience more complexity. If we let this complexity overwhelm us we will talk of stress, or at least of overload. With too many networks there are too many simultaneous relationships and contracts to deal with; life gets very busy while we get tired and irritable and curse the very idea of freedom and a flexilife. Organising one's life then becomes a major worry.

We do, however, have instinctive ways of coping with overload. The most common of them are listed below and may be recognisable to you. Unfortunately they are palliatives, not cures. They can anaesthetise us to the pains of overload but they don't solve the underlying problem; indeed they often make it worse.

THE WAYS WE COPE WITH OVERLOAD

Filters
1 Oversimplify the problem
Make it a black or white issue. Don't have any truck with 'grey'. 'Is she clever or isn't she?' 'Do you want the job or don't you?' 'Is it going to work or not?' 'Don't give me any ifs or buts'. (But the world isn't always so tidy.)

2 Let tomorrow wait
Only do the things which *have* to be done today. Put off consideration of the more difficult long-term problems and look at them when you have time. The future can wait. (But the longer-term things can be the important ones.)

3 Do as we did
Find a formula you used before which will fit this situation. 'Give her the old keep 'em happy routine.' 'Remember that X case. Let's do the same again.' 'My mother always said . . .' (But old ways do not always fit new problems.)

Escapes
1 Flight
Don't go to work (or don't go home if that's where the problem is). Go on a trip. Lock yourself in the tool shed or go to the pub.

2 Apathy
Lose interest in the whole problem. Relegate it to a third place, then you don't have to worry about it. Tell yourself that there are more important things to do, but don't name them or you would have to do them!

3 Drinks, etc.
Lose yourself in a good stiff drink. Or take it out on your husband/wife in a good row. A cigarette might help to take your mind off things, or even boost your ego for a while.

4 Illness
If none of the other mechanisms work then the body takes over and takes you physically out of action. Overloaded people are more prone to small illnesses like 'flu or backache as well as the more serious ones.

There are, however, two other ways of coping. Essentially, they are ways of getting the world back into perspective so that you can begin to deal with it properly.

Stability Zones
The term comes from Toffler writing about Future Shock. In all the trauma of overload, of change and of new problems we need to find oases of peace where we can regain our stability. For some people that is what the home is – a stability zone, while for others work is a stability zone amid the problems of domesticity. For some, strangely, it is the habit provided by the commuting to work, isolated from the world of problems in spite of being herded like cattle into a compartment. The routine of gardening, or of housework, can be a stability zone if you look at it positively, and not as a chore. Weekends, holidays, even business travel, can be stability zones for busy people, the age-old tradition of the Sabbath as a day of rest. If the husband comes home and goes straight to his slippers and the television, ignoring the wife and children, he has not necessarily got his priorities mixed up, he is just desperate for a stability zone.

We all need our stability zones – places where our identity is not challenged, where problems do not intrude, where someone else is in charge. If you don't have one, you ought to find one.

Meditation is an internal stability zone, if you can achieve it. It means finding a private mental state where problems and responsibilities are at rest. It is not easy, because it has not been in our western tradition for some centuries, but we can re-learn the method and the discipline.

Sport and recreation (originally 're-creation') are other possible stability zones; as long as you're not doing it professionally. It is here that golf and lawn-mowing fit in, not as exercise but as stability zones. No-one can get at you on a golf-course, unless you insist on carrying a bleeper, which will sabotage any stability zone. Instinctively, we all find some stability, even if it's the lavatory. Indeed, if you want to confuse and disturb someone then deprive them of any stability zone. Prisoner-of-war camps in North Korea and Vietnam knew this well, so do prisons and even public schools. Privacy, insulation from the cares of the world, security and, for some, tranquility, are the essentials of a stability zone. Choose yours with care. It is the energy reservoir in your life and needs cherishing.

Priorities

Stability zones are the positive equivalent of escape. Priorities are positive filters. If you can rank your problems and tasks in a strict order of priority you will know which can wait till tomorrow, which can be forgotten, which delegated. You will be able to say NO and to concentrate where concentration will provide the best pay-off. You will cease to be a puppet, jerking at the end of other people's expectations, but will be master or mistress of your own agenda. 'Time,' people say, 'if only I could manage my time, then I could relax.' Time is manageable with a set of priorities. Only then can you make the list of tasks for the time available, because you can cut off the one at the bottom. Any courses on the Management of Time (and such courses proliferate today) are, if you inspect them, courses on priorities. Some people make lists every week, or every day, but others are single-minded, and need no lists. They are lucky. Organisations call it Management by Objectives and stick numbers on the tasks, but essentially this is a disciplined, organisational way of establishing priorities. Sometimes priorities are forced on you, as a mother with a baby well understands, but we usually have more choice than we expect. It is a salutory exercise to write down at the beginning of the week the things to be done and then rank them in order of priority – the very act of doing this makes the week seem under control; the filter has worked. Put in a list:

1 The things I must do
2 The things I should do
3 The things I would like to do

Then allocate specific amounts of time to each, on particular days. If there is no room for the things you would *like* to do, have another look at the things you *must* do. Maybe some of them are not so critical after all. Take charge of your own time, be your own filter.

PHYSICAL WORRIES

How long do you want to live? What sort of body do you need for the life you are planning? How stressful would you like your life to be? More and more can you decide the answers to these questions for yourself and then deliver the answers. Health, Life and Liberty are things we do to ourselves, not things which happen to us. Anyone who has just escaped from a horrendous car crash or has become dangerously ill or seen a loved-one die prematurely will, rightly, reject the idea that we get what we deserve, but for more and more of us it is true. In youth one takes a fit and healthy body for granted. In one's fifties one has to work at it a little, partly because we have been trying to kill ourselves for years with the bad habits of civilisation.

105

How long will you live?
Start with the number 72

The following life-expectancy quiz is one of many health questionnaires now used by doctors, medical centres and insurance groups.
While quizzes can hardly be precise, they do give a more realistic picture of probable longevity than old-fashioned actuarial tables. In the
UK the average life expectation at 50 is a further 23.6 years for a man
and 28.8 years for a woman.

Personal Facts:
If you are male, **subtract 3**.
If female, **add 4**.
If you live in a town with a population over 2 million, **subtract 2**.
If you live in a town under 10,000 or on a farm, **add 2**.
If any grandparent lived to 85, **add 2**.
If all four grandparents lived to 80, **add 6**.
If either parent died of a stroke or heart attack before the age of 50,
subtract 4.
If any parent, brother or sister under 50 has (or had) cancer or a heart
condition, or has had diabetes since childhood, **subtract 3**.
Do you earn over £20,000 a year? **Subtract 2**.
If you finished college, **add 1**. If you have a graduate or professional
degree, **add 2 more**.
If you are 65 or over and still working, **add 3**.
If you live with a spouse or friend, **add 5**. If not, **subtract 1** for every ten
years alone since age 25.

Running Total

Life-Style Status:
If you work behind a desk, **subtract 3**.
If you work requires regular, heavy physical labour, **add 3**.
If you exercise strenuously (tennis, running, swimming, etc.) five times
a week for at least a half-hour, **add 4**. Two or three times a week, **add 2**.
Do you sleep more than ten hours each night? **Subtract 4**.
Are you intense, aggressive, easily angered? **Subtract 3**.
Are you easygoing and relaxed? **Add 3**.
Are you happy? **Add 1**. Unhappy? **Subtract 2**.
Have you had a speeding ticket in the past year? **Subtract 1**.
Do you smoke more than two packs a day? **Subtract 8**. One to two
packs? **Subtract 6**. One-half to one? **Subtract 3**.
Do you drink the equivalent of 1½oz. of liquor a day? **Subtract 1**.
Are you overweight by 50 lbs. or more? **Subtract 8**. By 30 to 50 lbs?
Subtract 4. By 10 to 30 pounds? **Subtract 2**.
If you are a man over 40 and have annual checkups, **add 2**.
If you are a woman and see a gynecologist once a year, **add 2**.

Cont.

Running Total

Age Adjustment:
If you are between 30 and 40, **add 2**.
If you are between 40 and 50, **add 3**.
If you are between 50 and 70, **add 4**.
If you are over 70, **add 5**.

Add up your score to get your life expectancy.

Adapted from the book *Lifegain*, by Robert F. Allen, Ph.D. with Shirley Linde, Appleton Books (a division of Prentice-Hall Inc.).

If you want to take more control of your bodily life, the rules seem to be clear, you must exercise, diet, and relax.

Exercise
This need not be the punishing masochistic ordeal that it sounds, although some find that the fifteen minute arm-stretching, muscle-bending ritual each day gives them a sense of conscious virtue. There are recommendations in Chapter 9 for any one who wants more reading on what might be called the exercise drills. Most people, however, will find it easier if exercise becomes part of the general pattern of living, rather than an extra chore. A walk with a dog is more natural than a bout of running on the spot. A regular game of tennis keeps muscles in trim more pleasurably than turning the bathroom into a gym. The problem with much of Western life is that exercise is no longer a necessary part of working and living. Like Churchill, confronted with the thought of exercise we can 'lie down and wait for the thought to go away'. Our bodies, however, need to be used. The more we use each part the better will we feel and the longer will we lead active lives. The research is clear. Vigorous activity improves our suppleness, strength and stamina, the three S's of a healthy life, and greatly reduces the chance of coronary heart disease. Vigorous activity means swimming, tennis, sailing, hill-climbing and dancing, morning exercises, heavy gardening or do-it-yourself outdoor activities like clearing scrub or laying concrete, major car-washing, brisk two-mile walks, running, cycling, climbing over five hundred steps. Golf and lawn-mowing do NOT count as vigorous activity nor does strolling to the pub (but they can count as stability zones!).

Looking at that list it is easy to see why some have suggested that if you want to keep fit in mid-life you have to be either rich or poor. The rich can buy fitness through sport and equipment. The poor have fitness thrust upon them, since they have to be fit to survive. The rest of us have to be more ingenious. We have to build a two-mile walk or its equivalent into our daily life if we don't want to end up like the man described by Richard Asher:

'*Look at a patient lying in bed. What a pathetic picture he makes! The blood clotting in his veins, the lime draining from his bones, the scybala stacking up in his colon, the flesh rotting from his seat, the urine leaking from his distended bladder, and the spirit evaporating from his soul.*'

Or this one, from *The Menopause Book*:

'*An under-exercised older woman ages more rapidly, more extensively. Her bones lose calcium more quickly and become fragile and her torso tends to bend forward as the spine softens and curves. Her stature decreases. Her cartilage hardens faster, resulting in stiffer joints and her flabby muscles cannot maintain good posture. This allows the normal thickening of her torso to be greatly exagerrated and her stomach protrude.*'

Diet

Diet is also a formidable word. It need not be. 'Tell me what you eat, and I will tell you who you are,' said Brillat-Savarin. A *sensible* consumption of food and drink can make life so much more trouble-free. We don't have to go in for punishing regimes of grapefruit or wafers if we work ourselves into a pattern that fits our life.

The facts are clear, and most people know them in the back of their minds. If people are even ten per cent overweight they are more likely to die from diabetes or heart disease, with slightly increased risks of pneumonia and damage to the digestive system. Even if they don't die, they are prone to arthritis, flat feet, and varicose veins – the discomforts of life. Two stone extra is, after all, the equivalent of carrying a small suitcase around with you all the time.

Animal fats, cane sugar and low-fibre foods are now generally accepted to be, between them, the principal causes of the 'diseases of civilisation' – heart disease, strokes, cancer, and bad teeth.

Ten thousand people each year are admitted to hospitals in England and Wales suffering from alcoholism (thirty years ago it was less than a thousand). Regular heavy drinking leads to ulcers, bad livers, weakened hearts and vitamin deficiency because one eats less. Alcohol is a major factor in accidents, both in the home and on the road.

Fifty thousand deaths each year are attributable to smoking in Britain. Half the adults in Britain still smoke although it is clear that at all ages smokers have a higher death rate than non-smokers, particularly from lung cancer, chronic bronchitis, and coronary heart disease.

The statistics are mostly about death. In some ways that is the least of the problems. If you're dead, you're dead and the discomfort is over. It is the discomfort and inconvenience that can make a misery of the Third Age. We do not *need* to punish our bodies by what we put into them. It is our choice and our responsibility alone, nor can we make the lack of information an excuse. There are enough books, programmes, and articles on what not to eat, drink, or smoke to keep anyone busy studying for the rest of their Third Age.

A list of a few of them is provided in Chapter 9.

Can unemployment damage your health?

'Yes,' says Professor Brenner in Baltimore USA. He has looked at the relationship between the age of death and various measures of economic activity over the last 130 years. He showed that after a lag of five years higher unemployment meant that more people died earlier.

'Not so sure', say Hugh Gravelle, Gillian Hutchison and Jon Stern of the UK who cast doubts on Brenner's statistics and believe that the evidence is still very uncertain.

Suicides did increase in the Depression years in Britain and are on their way up now. A larger proportion of suicides by men of working age took place when these men were unemployed.

The truth probably is that unemployment makes bad things worse. If you are poor, sick, badly-housed or suffering from stress your health will already be affected. If unemployment is added on top, it will make things worse.

The diseases of civilisation

(In order of frequency in each country)

Causes of death	USA 1980	UK 1976	Japan 1976	Kenya 1970
Heart	1	1	3	16
Cancer	2	2	2	14
Strokes	3	3	1	5
All accidents	4	6	5	13
Influenza/pneumonia	5	4	4	3
Bronchitis/asthma	6	5	7	7
Cirrhosis of the liver	7	8	6	18

Kenya's top 5: Whooping-cough, diarrhoea, influenza/pneumonia, typhoid, strokes.

J. Hendricks, C. D. Hendricks, *Ageing and Mass Society*

Is it not interesting how the top diseases in the UK are things we bring on ourselves, whilst in Kenya they are beyond the individual's control?

MONEY WORRIES

For many people the most alarming aspect of the Third Age is the money problem. We can do without a job, maybe, but not without the income from that job. 'Will there be enough money?' has to be the first question which anyone asks when contemplating a new life. 'What is "enough"?' is the real question. You may need more money for a new kind of life, but you may need much less. Our needs go up and down as well as our income. A *budget* which compares your income and your expenditure, before and after any change, is tedious but essential. The box on page 111 provides some headings. They all look rather obvious, but you may be surprised at what they all add up to and at the differences between one way of life and another.

The very idea of financial planning is anathema to many. It smells boring, dull, and predictable. It is better, some feel, to spend whatever it is that you earn – better still to earn what you need to spend. 'Let's go and earn a swimming-pool,' Paul McCartney used to say. Others find that way of life impossibly worrying. Unfortunately for those who like living dangerously in money matters, it becomes more and more difficult to adjust your income as you get older. More things become fixed. A few calculations will at least show you what room for manoeuvre you are likely to have.

The other reason for taking serious thought about money is that it is so complicated. If you don't go into it in some detail, you may well miss out on some very important opportunities, or pay penalties you did not know existed. Many of us are financial simpletons. We lose out through naïvety or ignorance not because we are cheated. We resign just when we were about to be made redundant with a big cash sum.

Do you, for instance, know:
1   What your pension will be? Will it be index-linked?
2   What social security payment you are entitled to?
3   What early retirement options exist for you?
4   Whether you will be entitled to a supplementary pension?
5   What sort of redundancy terms you can expect to get it if ever happens?
6   What opportunities exist for you to invest in a private pension scheme?
7   What expenses are allowed against tax for part-time work?
8   What is the most profitable place to put your savings?
9   What loans have tax advantages?
10 What grants are available for insulating your house?
11 How to spread out your bills for gas, electricity, etc?
12 What help you can get to start your own business?
13 How to buy an annuity – how to calculate whether it is worthwhile?
14 How to borrow against the value of your house?
15 How to make a will?

A budget

Income	Now	Then
Job		
Other work		
State pension		
Other pensions		
Investments and savings		
Other sources		

Total income

Expenditure	Now	Then
Taxes		
Insurance		
National Insurance		
Pension schemes		
Home insurance		
Life assurance		
Car insurance		
Any other insurance		
Home expenses		
Rent or mortgage		
Rates		
Electricity and gas		
Telephone		
Decoration and repairs		
HP commitments		
Food and clothes		
Food/drink at home		
Meals out		
New clothes		
Laundry and dry cleaning		
Transport		
Fares		
Car tax		
Petrol and oil		
Car maintenance		
Personal		
Holidays		
Tobacco		
Entertainment		
Presents		
Stationery and stamps		

Total expenditure

16 How to make sure your family pay no more death duties than they need to?

The answers to all these questions, and many more are readily available in books, pamphlets and from various advisory centres. Some are listed in Chapter 9. It is sensibly selfish to make sure that you don't lose out financially when you don't need to. The Third Age, however, does provide opportunities for thinking creatively about money. Have you considered . . . . .

Domestic import substitution

At the national level, import substitution occurs when we make things in Britain instead of importing them. The same principle applies to the home. There are many things which we could learn to make or do instead of buying them from others. If you learn to do your own plumbing, repair your own car, make your own furniture, you are indulging in domestic import substitution. Activity is moving out of the market economy into the household economy. Because there is more time available in the Third Age this kind of import substitution becomes more possible. It also saves money.

Home income plans

A number of insurance companies and brokers are developing ways in which one can take out a mortgage on one's house and turn that mortgage into an annuity to give you an income for life. No capital repayments are made until after death, the interest payments are taken out of the annuity but are, for most people, allowable for tax relief. It's a way of turning a physical asset into income without losing ownership of the asset. It makes more sense the older one gets. A seventy-one-year-old man could turn a £28,500 house into a new annual income of £1,312. Once this option becomes widely available it will make home ownership in later life very popular, because it gives you income with security.

Mid-life saving

Many people now have a small surplus of income in late middle-life when expenditure drops after the departure of children and/or parents. There are now several opportunities for inflation-proof saving.

Generation contracts

These involve the exchange of capital and assets for a guarantee of income from one's children. The rising generation may be able to make better and more profitable use of your assets, even including your house, in return for providing you with the necessary income. It makes you dependent on them, it is true, but it removes responsibility and can be a sensible and tax-efficient way of transferring assets.

Taking a lodger

If you now have spare space in your home, a lodger can fit in and at the same time provide income (which is counted as the wife's income and thus gets counted against the wife's earned income allowance for tax purposes).

Some attitudes to money

'For me, money means, I think, just money – not love or status or security. Nobody taught me to save money (my parents counted the pennies, and since I wasn't a big spender they didn't have to sermonise me). Nobody even taught me to spend it either, which means I usually spend without finesse, have no palate for it, though I do it as seems necessary. I know my money position is very precarious. But then I probably think that taking a regular job must be in some ways more precarious.'

'How much do I spend each year? I haven't the faintest idea. Why do you say that's stupid? Do you know how much sugar you use in your house each year? Of course you don't. Well, money is like sugar. I need to have some of it around, but I don't collect it, or consume it on its own, or even count it. It's got to be there but I don't worry about it all that much.'

'I remember the times when there was literally NO money – we couldn't go on the bus to buy food because there wasn't even the money for a bus-fare. You didn't have meals, you found food, if you could. Feeling hungry and cold was part of life, but I remember the shouting matches between my parents and worse the long, long silent evenings with no fire, no telly, no food. I said to myself then "I'm always going to have money" – and I have, but only now in my late fifties am I able to relax about it. It has been an obsession, I know that, but you don't realise how cut-off from society you are if the money isn't there.'

REJOICING IN THE INEVITABLE

Take care of yourself and your money as much as you will, there are still some things which you cannot avoid. In the long run, as Keynes said, we are all dead. Before that we grow inevitably older. Women go through the menopause. Men go bald, or bulge at the waist. We wrinkle, sag, and get out of breath. No amount of hormone treatment, face-lifting or aphrodisiacs will turn a fifty-year-old into a teenager. It is time to stop fighting and to rejoice in the inevitable. Who are we kidding anyway? The lock of hair placed across the balding patch deceives no-one except the man adjusting it in front of his mirror. We can no longer live in fantasies by the time we are fifty. We have to face up to the people we are, both physically and in personality. Depression is largely the result of comparing what is with what might have been. We have an ideal of ourselves, the people we could be, and we have a good idea of what we are in reality. If the reality is as good as the ideal we appear to be self-complacent, arrogant even. If the gap is too great we become depressed. A small gap is healthy, it gives us something to strive towards but we must beware of setting that ideal too high.

The menopause – myths and reality

'The menopause, or change of life, is as inevitable and natural as puberty. There is *only one* absolutely predictable sign (the end of menstruation). How each individual reacts emotionally to the menopause depends on many different factors; not only on the chemical changes taking place in her body, but in her own personality, how she has coped with the preceding years, the temperament of those around her, how she lives and what she wants to do.' In one American survey ninety per cent of the women interviewed felt neutral or pleased about their loss of childbearing ability. Only three per cent of women in a British survey said that they 'felt old' at menopausal age.

More women consult their doctors in the 22 to 44 age-group and 65 to 74 group than they do between 45 and 64. The long list of symptoms attributed to the menopause (insomnia, depression, headaches, joint and muscle aches, palpitations, dizziness, lassitude, absentmindedness, irritability, breathlessness) happen to other age groups too. Women in the American survey who were aged 25 to 40 ticked more of these symptoms than any other age group.

Fewer symptoms are experienced by women in higher income groups and with high education; unmarried women or those who have never been pregnant; those who had their last pregnancy over 40; those who started their periods late. Some women experience the symptoms over one year, others find they last for up to five years. Women who smoke have an early menopause but the menopause can occur any time between 39 and 56. Twenty-five per cent of women get no associated symptoms at all.

Sex need not change. As Masters and Johnson put it: 'The ageing human female is fully capable of sexual pleasure at orgasmic response levels, particularly if she is exposed to regularity of effective sexual stimulations'. Or as Princess Metternick replied when asked when a woman ceased being capable of sexual love: 'You must ask someone else. I am only sixty'.

Hormone Replacement Therapy is increasingly popular, particularly in America, and is clearly magic for some people giving them a new sense of well-being. But there are small risks of possible side-effects and HRT should only be used under proper medical supervision.

From Helen Franks, *Prime Time*

The fifties are a time for realism, for re-thinking our images of who we are and who we want to be, for accepting that fiftieth birthday as an opportunity not a danger, for rejoicing in the inevitable changes of life and the new possibilities which they open up. For many women the menopause proved to be a relief when it happened, not a tragedy.

Sex is another phantom worry. Will it stop? The evidence is that it slows down but need never stop. Is that such a disaster? Maybe the easing of the sexual pressures comes as a relief to some. There is as much joy and happiness to be found between 'passionate friends' (one nice description of marriage) as between 'partners in sex' (another description). Women constantly plead for more touches of companionship in addition to the squeezes of courtship. Maybe the fifties is an easier time for relations between the sexes just because the pressures of sex are less intense, less dominant.

Aloneness is another inevitability for many, particularly for women who usually outlive their men. But there is also the aloneness after divorce or after redundancy or the emptying of the nest. We can do something to make it less inevitable by better planning of our social networks, as suggested in Chapter 5, but for most there will be spells of aloneness in the third age which can easily turn into loneliness. It can happen even within a marriage. 'My husband and I don't get on. We live our separate lives within the same house and sometimes when people are incompatible they can be lonelier together than apart.' Mary the wife of a successful executive was describing her marriage (a C–C one).

But aloneness need not be loneliness. You have to start by not feeling sorry for yourself. If you are going to be your own company it's important to like yourself. Perhaps Chapter 4 may have helped a little. From that starting-point it is easier to go out and make contacts and friends. If you can be content with your own company then being alone becomes a treasured stability zone, the privacy you always wanted, doing things when you wanted, lying in bed late and going to bed early, cooking what *you* want to eat, not what 'they' want. Aloneness can be marvellously refreshing if it's your choice, when it is literally aloneness and not loneliness.

Death is the ultimate inevitability. It has replaced sex as the taboo subject in our society. Fortunes are spent by the state and by individuals on postponing it. The fear of it can colour our Third Age, turning us into cowards. Yet the evidence is that the closer we get to death the less perilous it seems. It is not death then that we worry about but the manner of our dying and the fear that we will be increasingly banished from our friends and loved-ones, left to die in a lonely hospital ward. The hospice movement has done much to bring dying back into the life of the community. It has allowed everyone to learn to rejoice in the inevitable, the family and friends as well as the dying patient.

The evidence is that dying concentrates the mind wonderfully – on two things – the future for those close to one and on religion or the meaning of life and, therefore, of death. Much of the time of the dying is taken up in seeking to minimise the hardships of those they leave behind. Old enmities often fade away as death approaches, so that harmony and forgiveness pervade. It is a good time for many, many people. Why then do we fear it so? Perhaps because we have not ourselves answered the question 'What is it all for?' Perhaps because we have not yet come to terms with life and therefore with death.

It is only sensible to be worried, as long as one remembers that there are worries *and* worries. There are some which we can do something about and some which, like the rain in England, you have to learn to live with. In our fifties, with twenty or more years ahead of us, there is much that one can do about the first set of worries. It would be only prudent to start right away if only because the actual act of doing something seems to put the worry in a file. The second lot? Well, when it's inevitable, one is always advised to lie back and enjoy it.

The things that are *not* inevitable

Go to your doctor if you have any of the following problems:

1   A persistent cough not associated with a cold, especially if producing a thick sputum
2   Breathlessness occurring more easily than before
3   Unexplained weight gain or loss
4   Swelling or lumps anywhere on the body
5   Change in bowel habit
6   Painful, frequent or poorly controlled urination
7   Excessive thirst
8   Loss of appetite
9   Pain in the chest
10 Painful feet
11 Visual problems such as pain in the eyes, double vision, seeing halos
12 Joint pain or stiffness or swelling
13 Persistent or recurrent pain in the abdomen, or vomiting
14 Giddiness, weakness, clumsiness, trembling or falling over
15 Bleeding, unless it is from obvious injury
16 Hearing loss
17 Mental symptoms: excessive anxiety, depression, gloom or confusion

From *The Time of Your Life*, published by Help the Aged, in association with the Health Education Council 1979.

 *C*HANGING

I once moved to a new job in a new town, which meant that at the same time as I was learning about a new task in a new world, my family were fitting into a new house and new schools. It seemed such a natural thing to do before we did it for, after all, it happens to other people every day, that it was hard to understand why the whole process was so traumatic, even, literally, soul-destroying. One year later we were very glad we had done it because we had learned so much.

This whole book is about change. I do not want to pretend that change is not difficult or, at times, painful, particularly when it is forced upon you. 'Change is not made without inconvenience, even from worse to better,' wrote Dr Johnson in the preface to his *English Dictionary*.

I do, however, want to suggest that change can be a way of learning, of developing new bits of ourselves, if we look at it positively. One piece of research, which was looking for the qualities that made for good 'internationals', people who adapt easily to other cultures and countries, came up with the finding that people who have experienced most change in their childhood, *and have survived it*, are the quickest to learn and adapt to adult life. So much for the belief that we should shield our children from all change! People can learn to learn from change. This chapter explains how it happens.

An agenda for my fifties

In reply to our request to look ahead at his own life, one of our respondents, Ronald Eyre, wrote: 'Now I'm in my fifties, and I face an agenda of what people in their fifties are expected to do. It goes, I think, something like this:

If you're on some career ladder, you're either at the top of it or stuck partway down.

If you're a parent, you're a grandparent.

If you're an athlete, you're a referee or, at best, a linesman.

If you're a handyman, you're less handy.

If you're a lover, you nod off.

Cont.

If you're a reader, you need glasses.

If you have opinions and tastes in music, clothes, dancing, they're likely to be yesterday's.

Just as earlier expectations were created to get the right, useful and convenient social effect out of you, the expectations for the fifties are created to ease you down the hill or into a corner. Well, in former decades I rather sought the corner. Now I have an urge to try and fight my way out of it. This involves a deliberate increase in the amount of learning and unlearning to be done.

At some points earlier in life, I took in and accepted images – mostly negative – of what sort of creature I was. If you can accept and act on one set of images, perhaps you can accept new ones. I'd like to learn if this is so and how to go about it.

I'd like to learn to play. By analogy with swimming it means letting one wave roll you, another lift you, plunging through another if you want to. Having a destination but not denying the element you live in in the rush to get there.

Some months ago, when I was in a very low patch, a friend of mine said "Don't worry. It won't last long". She didn't mean the low patch. She meant being alive. I cheered up immediately – particularly at the boldness of anybody wielding imminent death as a comfort. There's a real friend. What she did was wake me up to what big, long expectations I have and how disappointed I get if I think they are not being realised.'

EXPERIMENT AT THE MARGIN

Changes nearly always involves loss. It also involves risk. No-one can know how things are going to work out and some things won't work out. Any explorer knows that there are many false trails, while entrepreneurs expect some of their ideas to flop; statistically it works out that there are nine bad ideas for every bonanza. It's the same for oil companies looking for oil in new territories – nine dry wells for every one that flows. One has to learn not to take failure to heart. It isn't failure, in fact, but checking out another possibility. Science advances by systematically checking out all the possible consequences of a theory, expecting many of them to be dead ends. Those dead ends are not failures, only another possibility crossed off the list.

Living with dead ends is an attitude of mind. It helps if you are not risking everything on that one trail. 'Limited liability' was an ingenious invention which turned out to be crucial to the success of the industrial revolution and to economic growth. 'Limited liability' allowed the investor to limit the risk to which he was exposed in a new venture. He was allowed, by law, to draw a boundary around his liability. This meant that one failure did not necessarily ruin him. He had a fall-back position. As a result more risks were taken, more experiments started, more changes inspired, and limited liability turned out to be the oil of the growth machine. We each need to limit our own liability, for it is folly to stake all on one throw of the dice. Experiment at the edges of your life. If something looks like working, encourage it, build on it. If it doesn't click, then abandon it quickly before more harm is done. Water the seeds that germinate, forget the duds. This, as I see it, is the great opportunity presented by pocket-money work. This is extra work, marginal work, well-suited for trying out ideas to see if they make sense for you. If they don't you are not much worse off. If they do, then you know you have another string to your bow.

Exploring or experimenting – you have to put your toe into the unknown. Even though it's only a toe and not the whole of your body, it still requires a certain courage, even arrogance. 'Who? Me?' one is inclined to say: 'Surely other people have tried this already!' or: 'It must be illegal or someone would have done it,' or 'I don't think I'm competent.' Such humility is natural, but if everyone felt it nothing new would be attempted. Change does require a touch of conceit, of bravado, of self-confidence. It's another reason for looking for small experiments at first, until your self-confidence builds up.

Think of your life as two circles, A and B. B is the smaller circle and it sits inside the bigger one.

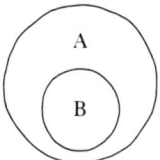

A is your total life-space. It is all the things you *could* do, the people you *could* be, the lives you *could* live. B is the way you see yourself now – you as you are now. They aren't really circles because no life is that neat or smooth. It might be better to draw them as very jagged chunks, one within the other.

The important thing about the circles, however, is not their precise shape but the nature of the lines that define them. These two lines are the boundaries of your life. The outside one, going around circle A, is a boundary drawn by society, by other people, and by your ancestors, who bequeathed you their genes. This boundary sets the outer limit to what you can do or be. You don't have the bone structure to be an athlete or a model, perhaps, or the fingers to be a pianist, the kind of intelligence that makes an engineer, or the temperament to be a teacher. These are fixed facts which you have to live with. They are one sort of boundary. Other fixed facts include the laws and rules of society, taxes, alimony, and the obligation to support yourself if you can. You can't change the climate, either, or the state of the economy. Your past is also fixed, the schools you went to and the jobs you did. All these put boundaries around your possible life-space, they define the outer edges of circle A, because they are the things you can't change. Circle A is fixed but it's big.

Circle B is smaller but it's not nearly so fixed. It can move around anywhere inside circle A. You can change the boundaries of circle B if you want to. You can move house, change jobs, experiment with new ways of behaving and different life-styles. The boundaries are the ones you set yourself. We often think that circle B is fixed when it isn't. We make up a picture of ourselves and think of it as permanent, as us, when in reality we could be lots of different people. The fifties are the time to play around with the two circles in your hand, defining the things which are fixed in life and the things which can be changed, experimenting with the edges of the circles, particularly the smaller circle which is your view of yourself. Anyone who has gone to live in a foreign country knows the freedom of being able to redefine themselves, far from the view of family and old friends, when no-one can place you by appearance, or accent, or mannerisms.

The saucer theory of work

Think of your job as a saucer – the kind of saucer which has that small inner circle for the cup to sit in, so that it looks like two circles.

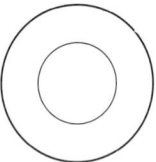

It doesn't have to be a very well-made saucer; in fact it helps in this analogy if it's a very crude pottery saucer with irregular edges and a little shapelessness.

Now apply it to your job.

The inner circle, or bowl, is made up of all the things you *have* to do in the job if you don't want to be sacked. These things are often written down somewhere, in an employment contract, an overtime or piece-rate agreement, or a job description. The trouble is that if you do all these things you still haven't succeeded. You haven't failed, it is true, but there is still something missing. You are meant to do more than just the things which make up the bowl of the saucer. You are supposed to improve on the printed list, raise the quality, make some new initiative, push up the targets, manage the group more efficiently, improve morale. You are supposed, in fact, to push out into the empty rim of the

Cont.

saucer to make your own mark on the job. The rim is not there just for decoration.

The problem is that no-one can tell you what the mark you make should be. If they knew they would have built it into the original list. You have to use your initiative and discretion. Success in jobs means moving beyond the centre. It's risky, of course. Some of your initiatives may be wrong. If someone sticks their neck out it sometimes gets chopped off. Experiment *is* risky, but doing nothing is riskier still.

Some jobs are all centre and no open space; there is no room for initiative, no chance to put your mark on your work. That is when work is drudgery. All centre means no fun, no success, no individuality.

Other jobs have very little at the centre. It's all open space – like someone sitting down to write a novel. There's nothing he *has* to do. That can be equally depressing. You need *some* centre to bite on but it should leave some space for 'you' in the outside ring.

LETTING GO

Change nearly always means letting go of something. Even when one moves to a better job or a nicer house there are goodbyes to be said to old friends, favourite routines or treasured landmarks that have to be left behind. If change is to be learning, a way of moving forward, we have to learn to let go.

The problem of letting go becomes most acute, of course, when a loved one dies, indeed the process of bereavement has been much studied. We think of bereavement in connection with death, but it is much the same in divorce, particularly if one of the partners is left unwillingly behind, or in redundancy and retirement, or even after a burglary or a fire in your house.

We know that most people in these situations initially go through a period of *numbness*. They don't really take it all in and either go into a state of shock and near-collapse or, alternatively, go on as if nothing had happened. It can be quite upsetting to friends to find the newly-widowed woman busily going on with her committees and shopping when her husband has not even been buried yet, but she is probably still in that state of unreality or numbness. The second phase is one of *searching* for what has gone. People who have had a leg amputated often 'feel' their missing foot for a long while after. The bereaved talk of seeing the dead person in a crowd, of forgetting that he's gone and setting the breakfast table for two instead of one. The redundant executive has, on occasion, caught himself getting on the train to the office which is his no longer. Then comes *depression*, when we finally come to terms with our loss and know that there is no going back, and after the depression, if we are fortunate, a *new life* which slowly emerges from the depression and gloom, as we construct a new way of seeing our life.

If we are to turn change into a process of learning we need to do all we can to help the process of letting go. Some things are known which can help. In the first place we need to be helped to accept that the past is really past, that the dead are dead, and the stolen jewellery really gone. That does not mean that we should put them out of our mind – far from it. But we should put them in that part of our minds which is to do with memories, the memories which make us what we are, but which are no longer with us. Separation before divorce is sometimes more difficult than divorce because the past is not necessarily past – it might still all come right. It was worse to hear 'missing believed killed' than 'killed' because one did not know if the past really was final or not. The rituals of grief are important here because they put the stamp of finality on a life whilst at the same time celebrating that life and so building it into an on-going memory. It is a shame, as I argued earlier, that we don't have more rituals to mark the end of things.

Continuity is the next key word. When we lose somebody or something a chunk of our life-space is taken away. We have to have some part of it to cling on to, for if we changed the whole of our inner circle at one time we wouldn't know who we were. Change the outer circle as well and we disintegrate, as happened to many people in concentration camps. This is the argument for experimenting at the margins, keeping your core intact. It is also the argument for finding another way to fill that gap in one's life-space which is now left. After a divorce people may or may not miss their departed partner, but there is an implied question-mark hanging over their ability to love and be loved, to sustain a relationship. It is the same with redundancy. One may have hated *that* particular job, but there is still that gap left by 'work'. Are we incapable of it? Could we live without it? These nagging questions drive many a divorced person to hectic amorous pursuits and the redundant worker to endless and almost random job applications. The gap cries out to be filled.

Continuity is also the explanation for our desire to cling on to accustomed things and ways even when all our good sense tells us we should change. It is this urge for continuity which makes us resist the reorganisation of work, however sensible or necessary, and which makes us resent new housing schemes even when the old houses are uninhabitable. Too much change cuts the continuity thread.

One answer is to look for continuity on a slightly bigger canvas so that the proposed changes look like experiments within a continuous system. Because big Japanese firms promise continuity of employment the workers will tolerate experiment in working arrangements, or will even transfer to new jobs and industry.

If the continuity of the *community* is guaranteed one can tolerate the replacement of a few houses, which feels like experiment at the margin. People who are very secure in themselves find it easier to move job or house, because their concept of themselves remains unaffected.

The other way to provide continuity is to work on your expectations. Emigrants who found their new country very different from what they had pictured had a rough time, because their sense of continuity was interrupted. Those who found what they expected flourished, because there just was not so much alteration to their view of the world, to their life space. The most practical way to stop change from hurting too much is to look ahead to the new land and find out as much about it as you can.

Continuity under difficulties

Bruno Bettelheim has described how prisoners in a Nazi concentration camp reacted to circumstances which were made deliberately unpredictable. The camp guards were deliberately capricious. A man might be punished if he did not do what he was told, but equally he might be punished if he did. Eventually, most personalities disintegrated under this constant barrage of unpredictable change, falling into an apathy which extinguished life. Exceptions to this were the two most ideologically dogmatic groups in the camp – the Communists and the Jehovah's Witnesses, who had their own form of continuity. Peter Marris* points out that the other exception was Bruno Bettelheim himself, who by understanding what the guards were trying to do was able to predict their behaviour. His understanding provided continuity.

Peter Marris also described how the Victorian missionaries in Africa managed to cope with very dangerous and unpredictable circumstances, surrounded by customs of human sacrifice and infanticide which revolted them. Many died after a few years from disease. Yet their journals are remarkably serene. They seem always to have been sure of what they were doing, however great their day-to-day disappointments.

*See Peter Marris, *Loss and Change*

PLANNING TO CHANGE

Knowing what you want is one thing, making it happen is another. There are, however, ways of helping yourself to change. One has the pretentious title of Force-Field Analysis. The title makes it seem more complicated than it is. In fact it is just a device to help you list all the things you have going for you and all the constraints working against you.

It looks like this:

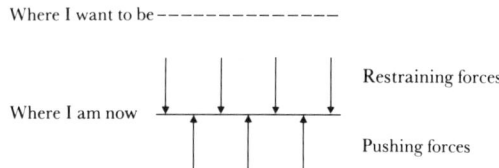

Where I want to be -- -- -- -- -- -- --

Where I am now

Restraining forces

Pushing forces

First you must define how or what you want to change; then you list those things which could *help* the change and those things which might *stop* it. If the list on top of the line is too big you will be getting deeper into your rut. If the list at the bottom is bigger then you are poised for a new life. If the lists are roughly equal you can feel frustrated, because the pressures below the line are being thwarted by the pressures above the line. To get rid of the frustration you have either to build up the bottom forces until they are irresistible, or to get rid of some of the things on the top which are holding you down.

Most people find when they do these lists that it is easier to get rid of some of the things on the top. Things that we think of as constraints are often not as fixed as we think they are. They are boundaries which we have accepted but which are not really necessary – they are the lines around the smaller circle (B), not the larger one.

A middle-aged sales executive, unexpectedly redundant, went to a counsellor with the list of problems and pressures presented below. He did not see how he was going to continue without his well-paid job because of all the commitments he felt he had.

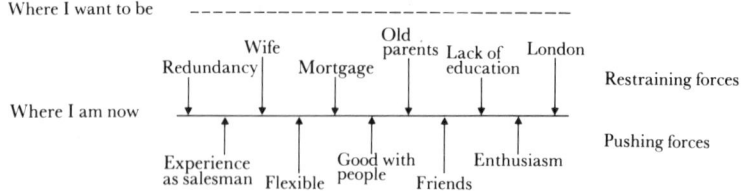

Where I want to be

Where I am now

Redundancy   Wife   Mortgage   Old parents   Lack of education   London   Restraining forces

Experience as salesman   Flexible   Good with people   Friends   Enthusiasm   Pushing forces

It turned out that his long-time dream was to own and manage a small orchard. Suddenly the expensive London house became a saleable asset, realising enough after their mortgage had been repaid to buy a nice house in Herefordshire. The redundancy, instead of being a liability, gave him enough money to pay the first year's costs of renting and stocking a piece of land. His aged parents, instead of being useless in London, found they could do little things to help in the

124

country. The London life-style, with all its expenses, just disappeared and was not missed, particularly by his wife, who now had a husband at home instead of an absentee salesman. The restraining forces disappeared allowing the pushing forces to come through triumphantly.

The secret lay in his ability to say where he wanted to get to. He knew how he wanted to move his B circle. Not all of us are as clear as he was. Some of the exercises suggested in Chapter 4 may help, if you decide to do them, but it is time now to become a little more specific and think about the diagram of the forces in more detail. Where do you want to be? What do you want to change? There will almost certainly be more than one answer, because you will have more than one ambition. For instance, you will have ambitions for:

1 Work (of all three types) – what sort of work would you like to be doing?
2 Relationships – what sort of networks of family and friends do you want to build up?
3 Personality – what kind of person do you want to be?
4 Material possessions – what kind of house, garden or other possessions do you hanker after? What could you do without?

Each ambition will need its own diagram of helping and hindering forces. To draw the diagrams, list, separately:
1 The obstacles in the world you will need to change
   Shortcomings in yourself
2 These go on top of the line, as the restraining forces; then
3 Actions you could take yourself – building on your own abilities and energies
4 Help you will need from other people, or other sources

The Force-Field Analysis has now become a plan of action. Add the plans together and you have some idea of the changes you have made to that inner circle which is you. You have started to shift it to another part of your possible life-space. All that is needed now is to put the diagram to work by attacking the Obstacles and Shortcomings on the top of the line and doing something about the Actions and Help below the line.

To do this you will need some *deadlines*. It is easy, as we all know, to draw up grand resolutions and then put them away until the next New Year's Eve. To make the action plan work you must commit yourself to action by particular dates. For the plan to work, however, it has to be one that other people know about – in a small way it has to be a *public* commitment. The principle is understood well by groups like Weightwatchers and Alchoholics Anonymous who also want to make sure that resolutions turn into action. They make sure that the resolution is not kept private but is a commitment which other people know about – your own pride and self-respect then keeps you up to the mark.

Jill moved from full-time into part-time work with her very understanding and helpful firm, to allow her to develop her own interest and business in making and repairing violins. She wrote this account of her experience:

Gestation time
'It took about two years from the time I first had the idea to the time I left my firm to go to the Technical College. I suspect lead times for most colleges would be worse than the one year I had to wait to get into mine.

Preparation
I took up a lot of top executive time and a lot of behind-the-scenes counselling, discussing options and arrangements. Anxiety made me take up more than was necessary. However the edge was taken off my worries by having the promise of a part-time job when I returned two years later. Financial worries didn't exist, thanks to the firm's amazing generosity in paying one year's salary while I was away.

College
I loved it. No problems with my fellow-students. I and another mature student acted as agony aunties for the others. The staff, after initial shock 'There's two old ladies in the violin room!' rallied nobly. I started with the rather childish expectation that I could sit back and be taught everything, but once I accepted that it was up to me to educate myself from the resources available, I got along fine.

It helped to realise that a more organised place would never have taken me. My main regret: that I hadn't done more woodwork before I went there. I had to concentrate on basics when I should have been taking in finer points.

Keeping in Touch
My new life was so absorbing that I felt there was a real danger of alienation from my old firm. So I made sure of dropping in at least once every holiday and at half-terms. Even so, I think two years was a dangerously long time to be away. Loyalty and sense of belonging both fell away badly during the second year. I feel, looking back, that a year would have been a more sensible gap from their point of view.

Re-entry to my firm
I was expecting my return to be smooth and without culture shock. It wasn't. I had banked everything on being able to do my new job in half of every day, with half a secretary, whereas my predecessor had done it full-time with a full-time secretary. I found myself with a completely new Department Head, who didn't know me, and expressed extreme scepticism that the job could be done safely part-time. I suffered a lapse of confidence, and for the first three months felt terrible.

Cont.

126

However, it turned out that my original estimate was right. In fact I'm able at the moment to do without a secretary altogether. So my job life is now busy but free of stress. (It's the first job I've ever had that I'm really able to do!)

I feel that the restricted time I am at work, and the need to leave everything so that everyone can see at a glance what is happening, makes me work much more efficiently than I would if I were there all the time. Perhaps a knowledge of how lucky I am – and how comparatively dispensable part-timers are – makes me extra-careful not to give grounds for complaint.

The new career

Thank God I didn't know when I started how difficult violin-making and repair are. I just sailed in with sublime confidence that I would be able to learn how to do it. Luckily it looks as though I will get to a decent competence.

But I definitely miscalculated the market. You *can* make some kind of a living as a local repairer, but only if you are fantastically fast, and maybe a bit of a botcher. I'm slow and a perfectionist, so without my part-time job I'd be in the soup. Luckily, with the job I don't have to worry about working uneconomically. I can just enjoy the work, and I don't have to feel I am taking bread out of other repairers' mouths.

On the credit side, the work is fascinating. It has been incredibly rejuvenating for me. At a time of life when a lot of people are suffering a kind of interest slump, I'm so interested that I don't have time to be bored or ill. But it *is* stressful, particularly as I know I need much more training than I've had to do highly skilled operations on other people's instruments, usually working against time.

Conclusions

From my point of view, I have exchanged a stressful job for a peaceful one; and a peaceful hobby for a stressful home-based business. But my mid-life change has provided a very high degree of interest, and an income-adding occupation which should last me until I'm too ancient to hold a tool. So retirement has ceased to look as though it will be any problem at all.'

PREPARING THE GROUND

Only the fool-hardy jump into a lake without first testing the temperature of the water and seeing how deep it is. Testing becomes much more crucial when you are doing something unusual. The steps one needs to consider are all very obvious. It's amazing that people miss them out so frequently. The reason must be that our jumps into change are *not* always planned, deliberate affairs. More often than not, we get forced into change. Few people *plan* to become redundant. Few people *plan* to get divorced. They may think about it but the thought goes away until one day the marriage becomes intolerable and someone walks out of the door.

This whole book is a plea for less jumping and more planned stepping. Paddle before you swim, think before you leap, know something about what you are getting into, in order to get some continuity into change. In other words do some *research*. Research sounds very academic and literary, and indeed some of it does need to be done at the public library. Your financial rights, for instance, can be worked out by reading pamphlets. The Yellow Pages are a very good way of sizing up the competition if you are thinking of going into business. The list of courses and classes is at the public library, so are whole shelves of books on keeping fit, eating well, or growing old gracefully. Whatever your interests you are bound to find a journal or magazine devoted to that topic. If you find that sort of research boring and difficult, do not despair – so do most people. Books are best as back-up. People make the best guides for your first tour of a new place. The second time take the book and go on your own. Find someone, therefore, who has done it all before. The great advantage of classes and courses is not the material in the course outline but the people who are there, the blend of experience which they represent. Some of them will have walked part of the way ahead of you. Pick their brains and learn from their experience, then check it with the books. If you are moving house, talk to people who live in the area you are thinking of moving to. If you are starting your business talk to someone in the trade already, preferably outside your area so that you are not competing (trade fairs and markets are good places for making these contracts, and most people adore the chance to talk about their work). Your tax inspector, if you find out who he is, will often turn out to be an excellent financial counsellor – for free! The country is littered with groups and societies and associations who exist entirely to support each other and to exchange experience whether it be on being a lone parent, collecting china, or growing asparagus. The very minimum of research in the library will tell you where they are. Write to the editor of the relevant magazine stating your problem. There is no shortage of people who are eager to share their experience and do your research for you. At the very least they will alert you to the questions you need to answer – then it's back to the books, but this time looking for specific answers to specific questions.

It is important to reconnoitre the ground before a battle, but even more important are some *allies*. It is best not to go swimming in strange waters on your own. If you can, try to organise part of the network you need in advance. It is not always possible, because change is often forced upon us. If you are going into pocket-money work think of doing it in partnership. The partnership may not last for ever or for long but the companionship it provides in the early days will be invaluable. Death, redundancy, and divorce, each present us with a sudden need for allies. No one should be shy about looking for them for it is normally pleasing and flattering to be asked for support. Receiving it is more difficult. It may be more blessed to give than to receive but it is far more awkward to receive than to give. Look for allies in unexpected places. In a new business your suppliers will be on your side and can be very helpful. Official bodies, too, like the Water Authority or the Electricity Board much prefer to receive requests for advice than complaints. We need to remember that bank officials make their living by giving financial help and advice and only charge for it when the money changes hands. Then there are brokers of all types. In the insurance and mortgage world they will actually be called brokers, but estate agents, heating consultants and shop assistants are all brokers – their job is to make a deal between you and the supplier of the service or the product. The important thing to remember is that they get their money from the supplier when the deal is made, not from you. Until the deal is made they are your free consultants. Use them as your allies and your research staff, bearing in mind, of course, that they are not always, or ever, completely impartial.

Allies seldom come to you. You have to approach *them*. If you are more of an introvert than an extrovert, more Apollonian or Dionysian than like Zeus or Athena, you will find this difficult. Discipline yourself. If it is difficult to approach them personally or by telephone, write a letter, but use the letter to ask if you can come to see them or they to come to see you because personal communication is the only way to form allies. Typewriters talking to typewriters or, worse, computer to computer, make no bonds.

Allies
Job Change Project
For the Unemployed Over Forties. A joint venture of the Birmingham Settlement and the City of Birmingham Polytechnic.

Background
This project was designed as a response to the increasing numbers of middle-aged people who were facing unemployment, often for the first time and with decreasing hope of finding another job quickly. It aimed to foster among the unemployed a more co-operative approach to the task of finding a job or of exploring retraining opportunities. A unit was established in January 1980 which included secretarial and social facilities, offering free typing, photocopying, telephone and video-TV interview training. From these small beginnings, a sophisticated agency service has been established with a registered membership of over six hundred and a success story of over one hundred jobs filled.

Cont.

The Think-Tank

It was early recognised that, valuable as the Job-Finding Service was, there was a greater need to create new jobs. The Think-Tank was established to explore new product development and to help individuals who were interested in self-employment. Its membership contained a cross-section of design, production, marketing, and financial skill. A small development fund was established to support prototype and other development costs.

Voluntary service

Since the summer of 1980 there has been a distinct drop in the number of vacancies available generally, and this is reflected in the Job-Finding Service. An increasing number of unemployed people are showing an interest in using their skills and experience in voluntary service in the community. Funding from the Manpower Services Commission has allowed the project to employ a 'Volunteer Co-ordinator' to establish a 'clearing-house' for such a service.

Associated Resources

An expanding group of unemployed men are offering their skills and experience to small businesses who could not otherwise afford such necessary services.

LEARNING TO LEARN

Learning does not only happen in school. If you think of all the things you do well, in the home, at work, in the sports club, or in the community, how many of them did you learn to do at school? Where do young mothers learn to look after their babies or managers to manage? Not at school, but on the job.

Asked to reflect on a major learning experience in their lives, people seldom mention a school or a college or a course. They talk of times when they were suddenly 'up against it' or 'out of their depth' or 'chucked in at the deep end'; change situations, in other words. Learning turns out to be about developing new skills, competence and attitudes to meet new situations. Of course, we need some basic knowledge to do all that and for some of the skills we need a lot of knowledge. Classrooms and books and examinations have their value. They provide a base, but that's all they can provide.

Change inevitably means more learning because once again we are 'up against it'. It is because the eighties are going to confront many of us with new situations that we will have to start learning again, if we have ever stopped. Learning is a very natural process – otherwise few of us would have survived thus far – but we can help it along a bit if we understand what is happening.

The basic process is very simple. All learning starts with a *question* which you ask yourself. It may be a simple question of fact. 'Which is the nearest town?' It may be a question about 'how', 'how do you control this machine?' It may be a question of 'what', 'what am I trying to do with my life?' The question drives you to find an *answer*, or at least a possible answer. You may find the answer in a book, or from another person, or maybe it has to come from within yourself. But you still have to *test* that the answer works in practice. If it does you have learned something. If it does not work you have to go through the process once again. The process then looks like this:

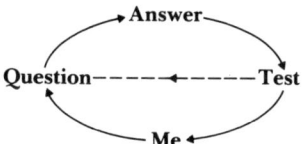

Diagrams don't mean much until you start to work with them. This diagram looks very simple and obvious *but* in practice the flow of learning gets blocked very often. Let us look at some of these blocks because, if you want to learn quickly and well in a new situation you need to make sure that none of the blocks apply to you.

Block 1
We don't see the questions. We have no natural curiosity or we are so bludgeoned by fate that we can only see one question, 'Why did this have to happen to me?' which happens to be the most difficult question of the lot. Lively people are people who are full of questions. They don't have to ask all of them out aloud, but they are the people who say to themselves, 'Why doesn't . . .?' or 'What would happen if . . .?' or 'Why does he do it this way . . .?'

Our questioning habit, our natural curiosity, gets blurred if we lead a steady and predictable life. Routine raises no questions. That's comfortable until you are suddenly thrown into a new situation with huge new questions, only to find that you have lost the habit of answering questions for yourself. You have forgotten how to learn. It can be very frightening and depressing. The temptation then is to run for cover, to find someone else who knows what the questions are, and can find some answers for you. It is a flight into dependency, a surrender of yourself.

If we are to cope with learning and change successfully it is important that we keep our curiosity fresh, and experiment with new ideas, situations, and skills. Questioning is a habit easily lost, indeed it is often drummed out of us by our parents, our organisations and bureaucracy. People asking questions are a nuisance. 'Why don't they shut up and get on with it, do as they're told?'

Block 2

We have the questions but we don't know how to get any answers. That can be a very frustrating situation. The car breaks down. Why? There is no-one to tell us. The economy is in a mess. Why? No one can or will tell us. Life seems pointless. Why? Even the parson has no answer.

Answers do not come naturally. You have to go out and find them, or come up with some yourself. 'Feeling' people are often very aware of the questions (which is called sensitivity if you approve or trouble-making if you don't) but they often find it difficult to move on to finding the answers. You have to have the urge, to be motivated to answer the question. There has to be a sort of internal energy inside you. This is where allies are helpful, even necessary – to keep you searching.

Block 3

We get a possible answer but then we have to put it into action to see if it works. This is where learning gets practical. Up to this stage the process can happen inside your head. We can speculate about all aspects of life, including our plans for the eighties. To do something about it, how-ever, is another matter. That requires the energy to act, which is different from the energy to research the answer. If feeling people get stuck with the question, thinking people stop at the answers. Active people, on the other hand, get impatient with looking for answers and try the first idea that pops up. If it doesn't work they try another. In-troverts find it hard to move beyond the answer stage, extroverts don't spend enough time there and often get the wrong answer.

Ideally, we should be balanced learners and good at all stages, but few of us are. That is why small groups of people tend to learn better than others. There is more of a chance that their learning habits com-plement each other as long as you haven't got a gaggle of extroverts or a clutch of introverts. Allies are critical to efficient learning, which is why being taught by a computer rapidly becomes boring and sterile.

Computers can give you feedback but they can't fill in the bits of the learning process at which you happen to be bad. Because schools do not have much opportunity to test every answer, they tend to concen-trate on the link between question and answer. Even then, if it's a question in which you are not interested to begin with it is unlikely you will remember the answer, and, typically, many pupils don't. The temptation must also be for schools to concentrate on those questions which have fixed answers – that is, questions of knowledge. Other sorts of questions need to have their answers tested out in practice, whether they are 'how to?' questions or 'why?' questions.

Do not therefore rely on the school or college to help you too much with your learning needs in the fifties. They may have some of the answers but it is unlikely that whole courses will fit neatly into your set of questions. You will have to be your own teacher. It is, in fact, useful to think of it that way, as a course, made up by yourself, on which you are embarking. List the questions (which then come to be the topics or subjects of the course), against them put the places and people where you would look for answers, and the ways in which you propose to test the answers. Then look for the people to help you, the allies. They should be able to fill in the bits of the process which are difficult for you.

After that, be *patient* with yourself. You may not be quite so nimble, so mentally alert, so deft or energetic as you used to be. Learning to use new tools, to read text books or manuals, to do routine physical tasks like building a wall, may at first be more difficult for people in their fifties than for teenagers. The compensating factor is the urge. Older people should be more highly motivated than youngsters because the questions are their own questions, the ones they need to have answered. The Open University is continually impressed by the dedication of the older student which more than makes up for any loss of agility. Two psychologists at Queensland University decided to put this to the test. They offered to teach German to retired men and women from all walks of life. In six months fifty per cent of their pupils passed the equivalent of O level, a standard which children usually take at least four years to reach. The brain, we should be glad to know, does not seize up in the same way as our backs or our lungs, but it can get out of practice. Getting back into the habit of study, of keeping notes and making lists, may take time; but it will work.

Changing competence

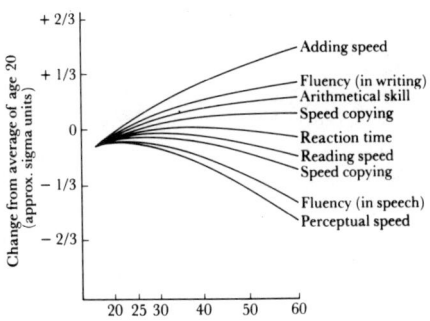

From J. Kendricks and C. D. Kendricks *Ageing in Mass Society*

The technical facilities for learning are going to be exotically increased in the 1980s – not because the government will suddenly put lots more money into education (it won't) but because business firms will recognise that learning is a growth opportunity for the new technological 'toys'. Courses on video-tapes and video-discs will become commonplace. If you don't own or hire your own video-recorder they will soon be found in all community schools, adult education centres, and even church halls. The Open Tech. will, in one way or another, become a reality – an open university devoted to technical topics. 'How To' books will continue to pour out of publishing houses – books are still very cheap learning materials. There should be no shortage of 'answers' available without any need to enrol in a college or university. But answers remain answers. You still have to provide your own questions, your own motivation, your own allies, and, of course, your own action.

It is tempting, in one's fifties, to pause and look back on what has been achieved. Work, a career, families, houses – whatever. Whether the view out of the back window is pleasing or depressing we should not dwell on it too long. There is still another third of life ahead. In that Third Age we won't be able to define ourselves by what we were, but by what we are. Historians, perhaps, or your grandchildren, will be interested in your achievements and your reminiscences, but no-one else. Living in the past is an indulgence granted only to the very old.

We have to move on. That means change, and learning. We do not have to be the victims of change. We can be its masters, influencing our own destiny.

A POET REFLECTS ON HIS FUTURE

To Be Dead

To be dead is to stop believing in
The masterpieces we will begin tomorrow;
To be an exile is to be a coward,
To know that growth has stopped,
That whatever is done is the end;
Correct the proofs over and over,
Rewrite old poems again and again,
Tell lies to yourself about your achievement;
Ten printed books on the shelves.
Though you know that no one loves you for what you have done,
But for what you might do.

To Be Dead by Patrick Kavanagh
Collected Poems

CHAPTER EIGHT

THE QUESTIONS FOR SOCIETY

I have suggested that there are touches of the inevitable about the 1980s in Britain. Traditional economic growth will be small at best. The number of conventional jobs available in the market economy will continue to decline even though the output goes up. We shall not be able to afford to make up all or even most of the job numbers in the state sector so that there will continue to be millions more people than there are jobs. Very many people will therefore find themselves with time on their hands, time which can, and often will, be put to good use in different parts of the informal economy. However, employed or not, all these people have to be supported, fed, housed, and kept healthy. Britain has since Tudor times recognised society's obligation to let no-one, however poor, be deprived of the bare essentials of life. To dump its citizens is not an option that is open to any civilised society today.

I have also suggested that new technological possibilities will bring some radical changes to the way work is arranged by some of our organisations. Organisations will become smaller, flatter and more spread out. Some won't really look like organisations at all – more like associations, clubs or co-operatives. Technological change has its own inevitability. You can refuse to accept the aeroplane for a time but the day comes when even granny gets on the plane to go to Australia – because there is no longer any other way of getting there. Resist technology as we may, at work or in the home, it is going to creep in.

The world is going to be different for many people. No amount of wishing will put the clock back. The message which I have tried so far to convey in this book could be summed up as: 'When the future is inevitable get up and enjoy it'. Now I want to add 'Get up and help to shape it.' We are not islands, alone unto ourselves. We are also citizens, voters, members of society and, in a democracy, have the ultimate authority over all the 'theys' who run our government, set the rules and staff the institutions. The changing future does pose big questions for society, questions which have to be answered because they are about money and people's lives but, unfortunately, questions which have no easy answer. They all involve choice because when the cake isn't growing very much we cannot eat our cake and still have it. Choosing one answer to each question means *not* choosing something else. Low taxes might be a popular answer to many but it has to mean fewer schools, or trains, or police. It is a zero-sum game. Anything I win has to come from someone else. In these sort of conditions it is *simpler* to let one person make the choices as long as everyone obeys. Dictatorships of the right and the left are simpler but they are not necessarily, or often, *fairer*. Democracies find it hard to find answers because no answer satisfies everyone or even most people. Even majority decisions are hard to get. So democracies work by compromise or the science of muddling through.

Our society in the eighties has some very unpleasant aspects to it, particularly for those who are young, unskilled, and underprivileged. Capitalism seems to many to have some unacceptable faces. The alternatives are equally frightening to others. If we are not careful we may see the opportunities of the future disappearing in the chasms of a society divided between rich and poor, class and class, left and right. An impoverished, divided, and embittered society would be a poor harvest to reap from technological and economic change. This book is not a political pamphlet. I have no ideology to put before you. What I do see, however, is a set of very practical questions facing us and our institutions. If we do not find an answer to them we will make all the optimistic possibilities of life in the 1980s and beyond seem like a wistful dream. I have picked out five main areas for consideration:

Money How do we make sure that everyone has enough to live on throughout their life?

Education Who will educate and train us and our children for the new society, and how?

Employers What are their responsibilities towards those who work for them and those whom they serve?

Unions What will be their rôle in a world of diminishing job-work and changing technology?

Voluntary sector How will this fit into the scheme of things?

These questions of the eighties concern *everyone*. They are the stuff of political speeches, or should be. They are, however, of particular concern to those in their fifties, partly because it will be easier to help yourself if society is pulling in the same direction, partly because it is one of our responsibilities to shape society for those who come after.

The questions are easy, the answers much harder. I can sketch out some options, but they are intended as an invitation to start making up your own mind, not as a coherent programme of political change. A detailed discussion of each paragraph that follows would need a whole book for each. Chapter 9 lists some which already exists.

MONEY

Traditionally a job has been a person's passport to society. Give a man a job and you give him money and the means of life. There are today in Great Britain 24.7 million jobs, but there are 56.0 million people. Most of the 31 million who don't have jobs are under sixteen or over sixty-five but they still have to live. Today, in effect, they are paid by the state in cash and in kind, through what I have called the redistribution economy. Pensions, child allowances, unemployment pay and supplementary benefit are some of the ways in which their wage packets come from the state. Problems, however, are on the horizon.

1 The Tax Burden

This is the issue to which I referred in Chapter 2. If the wage packet to the 31 million non-job-holders comes directly out of the wage packets of the 25 million job holders a vicious spiral is created. Higher tax burdens lead to higher wages which lead to fewer jobs which once again lead to higher tax burdens. It's the 'whisky tax' dilemma. Raise it too high, you cut the demand and get less money in total. It is also the 'divided society' dilemma with the resentful rich supporting the envious poor. Put the tax burden on the products and you spread the burden more evenly, wages do not have to rise and prices, net of tax, stay down. Income tax, as some put it, is a tax on employment, which must be crazy in a competitive world because it adds to the cost of the products. Why, they ask, can we not tax the result instead of the means, in other words the profits or the product and exempt those people we wish to encourage? If the product tax hits the poor too hard, then give them an income-tax credit. One could even go further than that and only tax their money when they spend it (as Professor Meade in this country and Professor Thurow in the USA have both advocated).

Tax changes are difficult because they always hit some people disproportionately hard and benefit others, but a shift away from income tax seems to me to be imperative if we are going to keep down the cost of work. Jobs are so expensive today that we have priced a lot of work out of society and a lot of goods out of foreign markets.

Secondly, the tax man has to learn to respect pocket-money work and not to outlaw it. At present all marginal work attracts marginal rates of tax, i.e. the top rates. No wonder we are tempted to try to dodge it, either by not declaring it, or by taking payment in kind, or by not doing the work. Pocket-money work has to be made legitimate if it is to grow. We have to remember that marginal or pocket-money work is not only a polite name for the black economy, it is also the work that

137

all of us would legitimately like to do in our extra time if it were not penalised so heavily. *Some* untaxed pocket-money work is already permitted – to pensioners and married women. It is not allowed to the unemployed or to the employed.

The problem lies in the definition of marginal work. We could, for instance, legislate for all earning from self-employment to be tax-free up to a certain limit, say £5,000 a year. This would apply whether one was a pensioner, a married woman, an employed or unemployed person. Since there would then be no guilt in not declaring it, one might as well declare it. This brings pocket-money work out into the open. Above that limit it is no longer pocket-money work and therefore taxable. Above that limit it is also more noticeable and therefore more enforceable.

Because much of the tax due on modest pocket-money work is not collected anyway the *actual* loss of revenue to the government might not be that great. If the change was accompanied by a move to expenditure taxation it could be picked up there, although the problems of policing an expenditure tax in the pocket-money area are as great as policing an income tax. An expenditure tax is however more understandable. All consumers pay it and the seller is properly acting as tax collector for the government. Evading the tax benefits the customer, not the seller.

It would be nice to think that the surge in economic activity which would result from legitimising pocket-money work would more than recoup the Treasury from any loss of income tax. It is certainly a hypothesis which needs testing.

The cost of change
Net cost of some possible changes in social security benefits in mid-1977.

Changes	Cost per annum (£ millions)
Raising Pensions to ½ average wages	2,000
Cut pension age for men to 60	2,000
£4 a week extra for over 75s	600
£10 Christmas bonus	100
Scrap earning-rules for pensioners	500
£1 extra child benefit to all children	600
Guaranteed maintenance allowance for single-parent families.	500

M. P. Fogarty, *Retirement Age and Retirement Costs* PSI Report December 1980

---

2 The Pension Problem

We have become accustomed to pensions, regarding them as deferred pay which we could have taken up whilst we were in the job but saved instead. The problem arises because we haven't saved enough, particularly if we all want to, or have to, retire early on the same money. Why, however, could we not choose to retire earlier on *less* money as happens in Sweden, for example? The TUC would like to see the men's retirement age brought down to sixty (as the French are now doing and as the Italians did some time ago) and the minimum pension level raised to half the average gross earnings for a married couple. The TUC calculated in 1980 that the additional *extra* cost of this to the rest of us would be £9 *billion*, or almost as much as the £10 billion we spent on the whole of the education service in 1980.

Although the TUC proposals are not out of line with those that already exist in other European countries they would almost certainly be too expensive to implement in one jump.

What we can expect to see are more pressures for the following:

1 A general increase in the minimum level of pensions, particularly for those (in their sixties and fifties) who do not benefit greatly from the 1975 Act which provided for the start of a pension scheme related to one's final earnings
2 Equalisation of the men's retirement age of sixty-five with that of the women's of sixty, probably by reducing the men's age
3 Better provision for flexible retirement, to mean leaving sooner or staying on longer, with pensions adjusted accordingly.

These will all cost money, money which has to come from other options as the box on p. 138 makes clear, because no choice is free. We, in a democracy, have to make the trade-offs.

There are major problems for those in occupational pension schemes whose pensions are paid by their employer. Should they change employer they lose out, essentially because the earlier employer feels little commitment to keeping up the value of the bit of pension left with him or to pass on enough money to the new employer to allow him to keep it in line with inflation.

It has been estimated that the first employer would, on average, have to put something equivalent to an extra year's salary into the pension scheme of someone leaving to preserve the true value of his pension. Few employers will feel inclined to pay such a generous leaving present if they don't have to. Few of us are in a good enough bargaining position to demand the extra from our new employer. 'If they don't have to . . .'; the phrase is an invitation for legislation to make top-up payments compulsory in order to allow people to switch jobs more easily, but a recent commission studying this problem came out against such legislation, believing that it would put too heavy a burden on firms.

There are other options, including a national reinsurance scheme, or even a pay-as-you-go arrangement which simply guarantees that funds will be made available by your firm to go on paying you after retirement, as the government does with the Civil Service. They all have one thing in common – they commit those in work today to pay for those who used to work as well as for themselves. A more radical proposal would do away with occupational pension schemes and require every individual to take out his own private pension scheme, with employers picking up the tab. This at least would make it easier to change jobs but would put the individual at the mercy of his or her chosen insurance company's profit performance.

The dilemma facing society is clear. A job has been a man's passport to a decent life. If we, society, cannot provide enough jobs for all who want them is there not still a continuing obligation to give him, and her, the means to that decent life? But at what cost?

Because we live in a democracy the answer will be a compromise. Anyone in their fifties would be sensible not to put too much reliance on the state-supported system meeting all their requirements for a decent living after sixty. Private savings is one route, but so is a determination to spread out the retirement process by more pocket-money work for long after the end of job-work. It is in society's interest that as many people as possible supplement their pensions for as long as possible because this lightens the total tax burden and keeps more money flowing through the market economy. Society, therefore, would be wise to relax the earnings rule on pensions and to encourage flexible retirement schemes, which will confront them with fewer painful financial choices than a big reduction in retirement age.

Part pensions

In 1976 the standard retirement age in Sweden was 65. Employees between 60 and 64 who reduced their working time by at least 5 hours but continued to work at least 17 hours got a part pension. It was equivalent to two-thirds of the earnings they gave up.

Over 200,000 workers were eligible in 1976. In 1980 53,000 were in the scheme.

A similar scheme has been proposed in Britain (by Michael Pinch and Ben Canolt in 1977). The idea is to create a flexible retirement bracket for both men and women between 60 and 70. People could choose a half-pension between 60 and 65 or a tax-free cash bonus of 30% official salary. The authors estimated that it might cost £1 billion extra when fully working.

Why 60? Why not 55?

---

3 The Income Dilemma

Should society support the poor or pay everyone a basic wage? As the box on p. 142 shows we currently do a bit of both. Even the richest households get on average the equivalent of nearly £1,400 a year from the redistribution economy, but the poorest get £2,500. Much of it is paid in kind, in the form of health services, education, and housing, and would be higher if the figures quoted in the box took into account the more general parts of the redistribution economy like the police, local government, or defence.

The support mechanism for the poor is bitty and complicated. There is national insurance, with its retirement, unemployment and sickness benefits. There are supplementary benefits, rebates on rates, rents, school meals, electricity and, occasionally, Christmas bonuses. You deserve a diploma in social administration if you are able to calculate your rights. Many can't and don't, so the system is inefficient. It is also demeaning. Many of the mechanisms are means-tested so that you have to put on a label of 'poverty' before you get them. They disappear if you get even a little less poor, hence the so-called 'poverty trap'. Between £40 a week and £74 a week, for every pound extra you earn you lose that pound in benefits. Even after that your net gain is only 25p for the next step. Because so much of the share-out (for that is what it is) of the national cake comes in kind, in the form of free services, one is effectively deprived of a lot of choice. You have to take a proportion of your social wage in the form of health, whether you like it or not.

It is for these sort of reasons that some people have for many years been advocating another kind of approach that pays *everyone* a basic wage, no matter how rich or poor they already are. This wage would guarantee everyone enough to live on, to cover, as it were, the over-heads of life. Income that you earned over and above that would then be taxed, so the rich would in effect have the wage taken away from them again in taxation. This idea has been given many names – social wage (the phrase I have used), national dividend, citizens' wage, income credit, negative income tax. Its merits lie in its *simplicity* (it would replace at one stroke the complicated array of measures) because as soon as your earnings dropped below a certain limit they would be made up to the minimum again; in its *fairness* because everyone, male and female, rich and poor, is entitled to it as a citizen's right: and in its *image*, because you would not have to queue or claim for it, it would come every week to everyone through the post or the giro.

What should the fifties choose? My own preference would be for an automatic entitlement to a minimum wage, indexed against inflation and guaranteed for life, to replace the system of benefits and, yes, even pensions. That guaranteed minimum wage would be a fall-back posi-

tion covering the essential overheads and providing the base for whatever job-work or, more particularly, pocket-money work which I
might want to do. My own preference would also be for as much of
that wage to be paid in cash as possible, because that leaves *me* with
more choice, and puts the institutions more into the market-place and
into reality.

The social wage
Households in the UK ranked in order of their gross income.

	Bottom 10%	11–20%	41–50%	81–90%	91–100%
a) Original income	10	270	4,380	9,360	14,040
b) + Cash benefits	1,720	1,630	530	380	380
c) + Benefits in kind[1]	780	680	960	970	1,010
d) Social wage (b + c)	2,500	2,310	1,490	1,350	1,390
e) − Direct taxes[2]	—	20	850	1,990	3,250
f) − Indirect taxes[3]	380	440	1,060	1,770	2,320
g) = Final income	2,130	2,130	3,950	6,960	9,860

Average 'social wage' for all households £1,710

No of adult workers in each household	0.1	0.1	1.4	2.1	2.6
No of retired people	1.0	1.2	0.2	0.1	0.1

1 Improved benefits from government expenditure on education,
health, housing, etc.
2 Direct taxes = income tax + employees' national insurance contribution.
3 Indirect taxes = rates, VAT, excise duties + employees' national insurance.

Social Trends 1981, HMSO

Note that households are 'rich' in direct proportion to the number of
people who work.

The idea of a social wage is not as revolutionary or as 'give-away' as
it sounds. Parts of it have been official Liberal Party policy for years.
The unconditional child benefit payments introduced by the Con-
servatives are in effect a social wage paid to families with children. At
present, as I have argued earlier, health, education, and other public
services are effectively a social wage paid in kind. A full social wage
would not only tidy up our whole social security maze, it would also
liberate a lot more marginal work once people felt that they did not
have to earn their whole livelihood through their wages. This, of

course, is what worries some people. Would the guaranteed provision of a minimum wage be a disincentive to full-time work? That would depend on the level at which the social wage was set. The Meade Committee took a figure of forty per cent of average earnings, at which level it would be unlikely to discourage full-time work but should encourage part-time, pocket-money work.

What *will* happen? Compromise, as is usual and necessary in a democracy. The benefit system will have to be tidied up but a wholesale social wage programme may be too complicated to introduce in the short term. For one thing, the money has to be clawed back in some way in order to be distributed. This means either a high rate of income tax on any earnings above the minimum level, and the Meade Committee reckoned it would need to be a fifty-five per cent income tax (leading to inflation). *Some* move towards the cash social wage is needed, however, if only to get rid of some of the anomalies in the present system. The box on p. 142 shows that the richer households get more in benefits in kind (because they contain more adults), and recent studies have shown that it is the richer and more middle-class families who make most use of the free services of the state, because they know how to get at them. That was never the original intention.

I said that there was no choice that did not have its cost, because to choose one road means choosing *not* to go down another road. That is why none of the money issues can be looked at on its own, or apart from the total situation. Any government who looked at the pension issue, for example, by itself would be appalled by the cost of lowering the pensionable age of retirement, or even of introducing some notion of flexible retirement. Yet, if one accepts even part of the scenario for the 1980s outlined in this book, it will be clear that pensions for people at sixty (or even fifty-five) is the other side of the coin from the dole and other payments for people from sixteen to twenty-five. The two populations cannot be considered in isolation because the whole working population is like the air in a half-empty lilo. Push a bit of it down at one end and it pops up at the other. You cannot get rid of it altogether unless you pull out the plug, which for humans means war or pestilence or famine. Society has to choose which end it wants to squeeze.

The concept of a social wage, paid mainly in cash, transfers some of that choice to the individual. If he or she is guaranteed a minimum income for life it is up to him or her to choose when and whether they want to top it up by working. The state then guarantees *livelihood not work*. In theory this would free up the labour markets because more people would be free to negotiate at lower rates, so potentially lowering the wages paid without affecting their final income. But if that was to work the taxation system would have to exempt the first large slice of earnings on earned income and the cost of that would be an increase in product taxes, which in turn would make life more expensive. There is, in other words, no such thing as a free choice in a complex and democratic society, any more than there is a free lunch. The questions are, firstly, who makes the choices and, secondly, what are the trade-offs. The issues are too important to be left to one group of people, even though they be our elected politicians. We all need to take a view, both for ourselves and for society.

EDUCATION

The emerging picture, as I have painted it, is one of increasing freedom for the individual. It is also a picture of increasing self-reliance or responsibility for oneself, which is the other side of the freedom coin. Conventional jobs in conventional organisations will fill less of our total lives. Even those who do spend all of their working lives in an organisation will find that they will be less closely supervised, will have more discretion, and will have to be more self-reliant. There will not be so many layers in the organisation, nor will it all be in the one place. Work is going to be more spread around, over the country and even throughout the factory. 'Get on with it and make sure it's good' will have to be more and more the management style. Work apart, we are all going to have more time for ourselves, discretionary time, both during our working lives and after they have ended. Whether we use that time for leisure pursuits, for part-time work, for voluntary work, or for the ordinary business of living, we shall have to do it on our own. No-one is going to bully or coerce us. It will be nobody's duty to see that we are making the most of our time or our talents. A great deal more of our life will be, literally, up to us.

Are we prepared for this more individual, independent way of life? Do we have the technical competences which are required? Can we type, prepare accounts, repair roofs and drains, work a chain saw? Do we have a saleable skill or expertise? I once accused a group of middle-managers of having been promoted to incompetence. Removed from their supervisory rôle what could they do on their own? They had no saleable skills other than their supervisory experience which was of little use outside an organisation. Do we have the personal skills we will need? Can we manage our own time, negotiate contracts, thrust ourselves into new situations, bring order out of chaos, influence people, and persuade them when we have no power or authority?

People in their fifties, particularly men, will often be unprepared for life outside organisations. There is a kind of conveyor-belt in organisations which carries one along irresistibly. Employees are not usually faced with great open spaces in the day, challenging them to fill them. The individual is paid for his or her expertise, while others do the bits which are outside their special area. Organisations channel people, turning them into experts or specialists, focussing them onto particular tasks. They do not breed and develop the all-rounder. That you have to learn outside.

The lost executive

Richard had had a successful executive career, finishing up as regional manager in the north-east. At fifty-four, however, he was bored. He would not get one of the big jobs in Head Office, he knew that, but he had done his present job for seven years, had done it well, and knew it inside out. The thought of going on doing it for another ten or eleven years was very depressing. He wanted to stretch his wings. The children were grown up. The house was too big. He had quite a lot of savings. He could afford to take a risk or two and start out on his own. He already had the promise of the regional agency for a couple of good products. If he worked from home the overheads would be insignificant and he could keep the commission as profit.

He took the plunge.

The business was there to be had, he found. It was the office side of things which bewildered him. For the first time in twenty-seven years he had no secretary to type his letters, answer his telephone, book his tickets, keep his diary, jog his memory, be polite to visitors, and organise his papers. The room he called his study was awash with papers. His diary was always in his other pocket. The phone rang and no-one answered; he got an answering machine but forgot to turn it on. He misplaced letters and missed vital appointments, typing was a disaster but his handwriting was worse and when the VAT inspector called he was almost prosecuted for evasion because no accounts had been kept at all.

His wife, luckily, found it all hugely entertaining. 'You've been mothered for too long,' she said, 'it's high time you learnt how to do the little things in life. The big decisions are always the easy ones. You had better go back to school again. Here's the address of the local college, they run a very good commercial course, I'm told.'

Where will one learn these things? Many can be learnt in the classroom. Bits of knowledge and information (law and accounting for instance), some skills (typing, book-keeping or carpentry), and some practising (of interview techniques or public speaking), are best learnt in formal learning situations where there is some input, some chance to practise with other people and some feedback on your performance. Other things can be learnt only by trial and error, by jumping in and trying in the ways outlined in Chapter 7.

Where should these classrooms be? In the colleges of further education? In the home? In the organisation? The colleges do a lot already, particularly in the technical skill area. Do they do enough to re-train adult people for real work as opposed to hobbies? Is education moving out of the classroom into the living room, through instructional books, tape-recorders and, now, video-tapes and video-discs. Cookery and gardening have gone this way. Will typing and accounting, law and carpentry be the next home-education area? Is business cashing in on the boom in learning for adults faster than the colleges or the schools? Should the community-school movement be pushed ahead, so that the facilities used to teach our youth are also available to our adults?

What about the employing organisation? Should it be part of its responsibility to educate and train its employees for life *outside* the organisation. In the Armed Services it is recognised that employment is seldom for life, but, in return, almost, one is equipped with skills which *can* last for life. 'Give a man a fish and you feed him for a day' runs the old proverb, 'teach him to fish and you feed him for life.'

And what about the youth? In our pre-occupation with ourselves in our fifties we must not forget the growing generation. Are our schools and universities preparing people for this more self-reliant life? Are they educating them with the awareness of the commercial realities of life – that bread does not come as manna from heaven but, in the first place, from profitable industrial and commercial enterprise? Are the examination methods geared to personal skills as much as they should be or do they still emphasise knowledge at the expense of capability? Is it right that forty per cent of our children should leave school without any qualifications at all? Who is to train them for the skills and trades of work? Why have we neglected apprenticeship so that sixty per cent of our youth get *no* further training at all after school, for, as far as can be seen, the rest of their life? Is the educational system now too self-contained, too insulated from reality to change these things? Should we leave it to the Manpower Services Commission, employing organisations with apprenticeship and work experience programmes, the CBI and the media to educate the young for life or should we seek to influence the educational process in the schools and universities?

These are important questions for those in their fifties for they are better placed than teachers to see which way the world is going and it is their grandchildren who will be in those schools.

Education for Capability manifesto

'We, the undernamed, believe that there is a serious imbalance in Britain today in the full process which is described by the two words 'education' and 'training'. The idea of the 'educated person' is that of a

---

Cont.

scholarly, leisured individual who has been neither educated nor trained to exercise useful skills; who is able to understand but not to act. Young people in secondary or higher education increasingly specialise, and do so too often in ways which mean that they are taught to practise only the skills of scholarship and science. They acquire knowledge of particular subjects, but are not equipped to use knowledge in ways which are relevant to the world outside the education system.

We believe that this imbalance is harmful to individuals, to industry and to society. A well-balanced education should, of course, embrace analysis and the acquisition of knowledge. But it must also include the exercise of creative skills, the competence to undertake and complete tasks and the ability to cope with everyday life; and doing these things in co-operation with others.

We consider that there exists in its own right a culture which is concerned with doing, making and organising, and the creative arts. This culture emphasises the day-to-day management of affairs, the formulation and solution of problems and the design, manufacture and marketing of goods and services.

We believe that educators should spend more time preparing people in this way for a life outside the education system; and that the country would benefit significantly in economic terms from what we describe as Education for Capability.'

This Manifesto was signed by over a hundred leading businessmen, educationalists and public figures and published in the Press in February 1982 as an introduction to an award scheme run by the Royal Society for the encouragement of Arts, Manufactures and Commerce.

EMPLOYERS, INDUSTRY AND BUSINESS

The primary responsibility of employers must be to get the job done in the most efficient and effective way. As far as industry and business is concerned that must put a priority on the profitability of the firm which is as good an indicator of efficiency as we have, although it does need to be looked at over the longer term and not in short-term fluctuations.

But the eighties bring other pressures to bear which point to important policy issues, issues which will be bound to concern those in their fifties:

1 The Job share-out

The issue has already been discussed in Chapter 4. I list it here again because of its importance and its urgency. At present employers have almost eliminated recruitment, thereby giving the reduced number of jobs (down by ten per cent in manufacturing in 1981) to their older workers. This is understandable in the short term, intolerable in the long term. Ways must be found to modify the 3×48 tradition of employment.

One company talks excitedly of the day when all its workers and man-agement will expect to leave at forty-five, not to retire but to find other work, in smaller firms or self-employment, with a capital grant or part-pension to start them off. It is a tradition already established in the Armed Services who hit the overmanning problem two decades ago. The company is excited because such a policy would open up the opportunity to put younger managers and skilled workers in the posi-tions of authority. Another company, this time in the USA, conscious-ly pursues what it calls its 'In, Up and Out' philosophy encouraging its people to move on to other work in their forties, leaving the road clear for younger people.

Pension policy is crucial here, but so is the resolution of the em-ployer. No long-term view could countenance the continued exclusion of the new generation.

2 Education and training

This issue was also discussed, in the previous section of this chapter. Can organisations afford to delegate education and training to the educational system? If they do not educate people to leave they will be stuck with an increasingly ageing work-force. If they don't educate and train the youth they will end up with unskilled workers – which they complain of today – because the educational system is not and never has been geared to serious vocational training. One could argue that it should be more focussed that way but no amount of urging will get schools and school teachers to do what they cannot do: prepare people in detail for work. Education for life is difficult enough, educa-tion for occupation is perhaps an unfair request of the normal school. Specialist vocational schools could be created, staffed perhaps by some of those in their fifties. Alternatively the organisation can be-come the school, again using the experienced older worker as the tutor and apprentice-master. Government funding can ease the costs, but the staff, and direction, must come from employers themselves.

3 Job creation

Jobs disappear and new jobs come; that is the unending process of change. The blacksmith gave way to the motor mechanic, and who then would have dreamt of car ferry pilots, service station attendants, and motorway cafés? Similarly who would be bold enough to predict the new jobs of 1989 or 1999, except for the certainty that many of them will be for lawyers! I have argued that no amount of job creation will make up for the jobs that go, but that does not mean that we should not strive to create as many new jobs as we can.

New jobs, however, do not grow on trees or spring by some spon-taneous generation out of virgin soil. We need not expect to see many of them coming directly from the larger corporations because these were long over-manned and today have the capital equipment and manning reserves to grow considerably in output without increasing the number of jobs. There will, of course, be piece-meal exceptions as economic recovery begins, but they will always be in hundreds, compared with the thousands leaving.

The exciting area for new jobs comes from new business, not old. Here the numbers are in tens, not hundreds, let alone thousands. They will not solve the unemployment problem, these new enterprises, but they are the business seed-corn for the future and they need nurturing.

Nurturing implies a little special feeding, shelter, encouragement and advice. Where do the new enterprises go to for this form of nurturing? To the banks in the first instance. But banks turn out to be better at propping up going concerns when they can see where their money is going than risking their shareholders' funds on new ideas and new people.

Perhaps this is where the bigger firms have a new rôle to play. They cannot create the jobs themselves but they could do more to act as godfather to fledgling companies, even as the 'secondary bankers' to the new companies. The idea is that the big companies know more about new businesses and managing them than banks do. The banks lend to the companies who lend it on to the new businesses, with some advice and monitoring thrown in for good measure. This type of intermediate institution already has its prototype in ICFC, which acts as a financial godfather to many new businesses and has a healthy track record of success. It needs more part-time imitators.

It could be said that the new phenomenom of 'management buy-outs', referred to in Chapter 3, whereby a company encourages the purchase of a subsidiary or a plant by its own managers and workers, is a godfather operation, but too many look upon a 'buy-out' as a painless alternative to redundancy rather than a positive planting of a cutting. Maybe they should change their outlook.

More obviously godfatherly are the Local Enterprise Trusts which are gradually appearing round the country. These trusts are alliances of local businesses and local government set up to facilitate new businesses. 'Business in the Community' is the new umbrella for this type of godfather activity and their *Handbook for Action* illustrates the wide range of small enterprises they and their sponsoring companies have promoted.

It is managers and skilled workers in their fifties who most appropriately fit this godfather rôle. Not only is the rôle good in itself, it provides a splendid stepping-stone for the godfather into his own enterprise. Nor need all those enterprises be commercial business ones. The voluntary world needs godfathers as much, or more than, new business. The jobs created may be gift-work not job-work but they are still valuable opportunities for human talent and initiative. Big firms must be full of potential godfathers in their fifties. For their sake and the sake of society they should be used.

4 Capital sharing

Firms, particularly business firms, are going to look more like villages, with their core of permanent occupants enjoying right of tenure. This permanence is today forced on organisations by legislation, legislation which will hardly be undone. Business has acquired its own rent act, its own set of sitting tenants. It is, in part, that sitting-tenant situation that encourages more firms to look for flexibility in contracting out, but there will always be a core of permanent tenants. Tenants can be obstructive and uncaring of the furniture and business would be wise to consider converting its tenants into co-owners. There is a growing interest in various schemes of capital sharing, and, inevitably, many technical problems attached to them.

Organisations see these schemes as ways of improving motivation, of giving their people a stake in the future of the organisation. For the fifties generation this is, of course, true, but they have another interest in the ideas. A capital stake in a business is a valuable addition to one's pension, providing income, the possibility of capital growth and the down payment, as it were, on a life membership of your old club. The Inland Revenue allows a number of shares to be allocated to an employee each year, with tax concessions. Fifteen years of this sort of allocation can build up a nice capital sum. There are risks, it is true, but some schemes allow the trustees of these sort of shares to re-invest the accumulated profit as some sort of hedge.

The idea of capital sharing is still at a primitive level in Britain compared, for example, with Germany. It is not yet a matter of vital concern to politicians, unions, or industry. The objectives and details still have to be worked out, but as a way of spreading ownership and investment it has many attractions.

Employees, particularly those in business and industry, have to face up to the fact that the employment organisation is, today, the dominant social organisation in our lives, particularly during the Second Age. Because of that fact no manager, director, or administrator can any longer shelter behind his own definition of his task or product. He is very much a part of society, one of society's villages, if not towns, and has to live up to the total responsibility involved. The fifties generation has a particular interest in seeing that this happens for they will be the most immediate beneficiaries, or victims if it goes wrong.

THE UNIONS

The unions have a rôle and a choice in the picture for the eighties. They can continue in their chosen rôle as pay-brokers, negotiating the best deal possible for their members. Given the British preference for arriving at compromise by setting up two opponents to batter away at each other, there will almost certainly be a continuing need for the unions as champion of the employees in the annual pay tournament. Yet if they stick to this narrow definition of their rôle they will not only find themselves with a declining market (as employment drops) but will also miss out on the chance to influence a changing world. Not only that, they will be inadequate champions of the working man in all his or her different guises, for work, as this book has tried to demonstrate, will not be confined to the insides of organisations.

The unions have several options for going beyond 'pay and conditions'; but all the options require a readiness to accept that the world is going to be a little different. Firstly, they can engage in the re-allocation of the three forty-eights. The reduction of overtime, and the reduction of the working week are already part of the TUC programme but because they are combined with a determination to keep existing earning levels they will not, in fact, redistribute work. If employees can do the same work for the same money in less time the only effect is to give those employees more time. True re-allocation has to involve a reduction in pay. This is more likely to become a reality when we look at years rather than hours or weeks. Lower pensions for early retirement or lower pay for trainee workers are more likely to be negotiable than lower rates per hour or per week.

A fifty per cent youth wage, for instance, preferably combined with the provision of some training, would make it economic to employ more youngsters. Part-pay and part-pension for part-time would make it easier to keep on older people. If the unions seriously want to keep more people in employment they have to spread out the pay as well as the time and the jobs. Larger pay increases produce corresponding pressures for large productivity increases, which, in the end usually mean manpower *decreases*. The successful pay negotiator may find himself the herald of more redundancies.

Secondly, they can adopt the unemployed. At present the unions are in a dilemma. At the national level they condemn the unnatural and, they would say, immoral levels of unemployment. In practice, their pay-broker rôle forces them to give priority to those who have jobs. Their support of the unemployed is token at best. This is partly because many unemployed leave the union when they leave unemployment. Dues become too expensive. It is partly because the unions are not equipped to do much for the individual unemployed except to plead their case in the national forum. More concern with re-equipping and re-training and relocating the unemployed would be welcome. There are a few unemployment centres but they are hardly more than rest centres. An active adoption programme for the unemployed, as associate members with minimal dues, would help where it hurts.

Thirdly, they could champion the new defenceless. The growing army of part-time workers, the self-employed and the contract people are in need of help. The part-time outworker has always been an opportunity for exploitation. We may be cleverer today than the cottage-workers of old but we can still be exploited, and can still be confused by the complexities of law and tax and employment regulations. The self-employed in the professions have their associations, which are very similar to the guilds of yesteryear. They license one to practise (after an examination and apprenticeship) and fix scales of charges. Both practitioner and customer are thereby protected. The new self-employed will need their guilds. If the unions do not choose to move into this field there will have to be more state regulatory devices, as suggested in Chapter 4. Self-regulation is, in general, preferable to state regulation, but society, like nature, abhors a vacuum and the state, almost in spite of itself, will move into this gap unless the union movement sees this as part of its changing rôle.

Last but not least, they could welcome the new technologies. Technology, I have argued earlier, has a force of its own. Canute could not stop the tide nor can society stop technological change. To postpone it is to miss the opportunities that change can bring. Inevitably, technological change, like all change, involves loss, and in this case, loss of jobs. The trick is to prepare for spring in the midst of winter, by educating people for the *new* jobs. Unfortunately the structure of the trade union movement in Britain, linked, as so much of it is, to the old craft union, is not framed so that it can get spring and winter into the same vision. ASLEF's un-needed train drivers could find their new opportunity in electronics or even lorries. But those are not part of ASLEF's vision – they are stuck with the problems of winter without hope of spring. Japan was able to run down her shipbuilding industry without incident because the bulk of shipworkers were re-located by the same firm and the same union. It was like moving bedrooms not moving house. The structure of the trade union movement has to change as well as its attitudes. Canute was bluffing. He knew the water was deaf. Is the trade union movement bluffing, making noises for the benefit of the citizenry? We must hope so.

THE VOLUNTARY SECTOR

The 1980s are a magnificent opportunity for the voluntary world. I have argued that gift-work and pocket-money work are bound to increase. The need for more free and low-priced work in the communities of Britain is undeniable. At the same time the band of potential volunteers is increasing, particularly among people in their fifties who are still full of energy and talents. Can the sector meet the challenge? The effort is already considerable. In 1976 the Wolfenden Committee on voluntary organisations estimated that five million adults had done some voluntary work in the previous year, equivalent in time to four hundred thousand workers working full-time.

A more recent survey found that forty per cent of those interviewed had done some voluntary work in the previous year and eighteen per cent had done six hours or more in the previous week. That's a lot. It's important because voluntary organisations can provide the individual with some of those 'structures for mattering' and networks mentioned in Chapter 5 which are so crucial to an individual's self-respect. Properly organised they are also good for society.

The obvious scope for the increase in the voluntary sector is to supplement or replace part of the statutory services of the State. The lifeboat crews, the Samaritans and Marriage Guidance, to take but three examples, are already saving the state millions of pounds as well as providing an opportunity for personal service to many dedicated people. Could it go farther?

If it is to go farther the public will need an assurance of quality. No amount of goodwill compensates for incompetence or incapacity. It is up to the voluntary sector to see that its standards are equal to the best comparable professional standards and to put in proper training and monitoring devices to make this happen. It is also up to them to ensure that the management of their organisations is good enough.

The implications of these simple-sounding statements are big. They mean that not everyone who wants to do something can always be allowed to do it. They mean that dedication is no excuse for bad management. The direction and administration of the organisation has to accept the same kinds of efficiency criteria as other organisations.

To provide the professional and managerial core that is needed if the voluntary sector is to grow in the needed directions it will be necessary to provide more full-time or part-time paid jobs in the core. Gift-work is, by its nature, fringe work. Core-work needs the priority given to it which for most people means that it has to be paid. It is here that the partnership with the state could be expanded, with the state funding the core but not the fringe, and helping to endorse the qualifications and standards of the organisation. Voluntary organisations could be seen not only as a way of giving but also as a way of acquiring new skills and, if necessary, qualifications. Gift-work should be sèrious work, not casual work, if it is to have its proper and respected place in society.

The voluntary world

Did you know . . .?

Over 1.3 million young people belong to the Guide and Scout Associations.

More people (11%) go to church each week than watch football (9%)

The British Red Cross Society and the St John Ambulance Brigade are obliged to train any member of the public who has to have a first aid certificate as part of their work. In 1980 they issued nearly 141,000 certificates.

The WRVS served nearly 17½ million meals to elderly and handicapped people in 1980, and visited 22,000 people with their 'Books on Wheels' service.

The Citizens Advice Bureau had 4,367,100 clients in 1980.

The Samaritans had 298,600.

The Royal National Life-Boat Institution spent £9,700,000 in 1980.

There are 136,000 registered charities with a total income of £2,640,000,000 of which forty per cent comes from voluntary donations.

Social Trends 1981, HMSO

Room for you? Room for more?

IN CONCLUSION

You cannot solve new problems with old answers. The theme of this book is that the eighties is the decade of new problems. I have tried to suggest a few of the answers.

I have not, in this chapter, discussed new economic strategies or new political platforms. There has been nothing about monetarism or import controls or proportional representation, nothing about union legislation or Trident missiles, nothing about the Third World, energy, pollution, urban decay, class, or racial discrimination. It is not that I don't think these things to be important. They are important and they do concern us.

They are, however, well-aired elsewhere. They are not peculiar to being fifty in the eighties. They affect all of us, and they are not even, most of them, peculiar to the eighties, for they are arguments which have been going on for a long time in different disguises.

This has been a discussion of the things which *we* can influence or do which will make it easier and more useful to be fifty in the eighties. There are many who say 'Get the big things right, like wars and the economy, and the rest will fall into place'. They have simple answers to complicated problems. 'Government investment will put the world back where it was.' It won't. It might help a little but it won't make all the problems disappear. It will *still* be different to be fifty in the 1980s because so many other things have changed, for ever, as well as the economy and the price of oil. It cannot be the same again, whatever government and whatever they decide.

We cannot, therefore, leave it to governments. If war is too important to be left to generals, life is too important to be left to politicians. This book has concentrated on the things that we, in our fifties, can do. Some of them may seem small things set against the great dramas of the world but, cumulatively, they are not. Great houses are built from single bricks. We have to think both about the sort of house we want to live in and do something to create the bricks. That way we can have a satisfying future for ourselves and do something to ensure that there is also a future for those who come after us.

For those of us in our fifties today that future may be very different from the one we had come to expect. It will have its dangers, to be sure, but also its opportunities. We need to concern ourselves with both.

155

CHAPTER NINE

ESOURCES

This book is designed to be a sketch-book etching in the scenery we may expect to find in the 1980s and the ways that we have of adapting to the kinds of changes we may encounter. Each chapter could justify a whole book in itself and indeed many of those books already exist. For those who want to take any topic a little further, this chapter will tell them how to get started. I have not attempted to list all the publications or organisations concerned with each topic. The list would daunt even the most ardent searcher after truth. Instead, I have listed two or three recent publications and some knowledgeable organisations. They will in turn lead you to others, like a tracker following a trail. The publications should all be accessible, either from the publisher, or from a good bookshop, or from your local library. The organisations will respond to a telephone call, and all have their own literature.

CHAPTER ONE
THE NEW QUESTIONS

Catastrophe has not been the theme of this book, but the possibility of catastrophe needs to be taken seriously by everyone. An excellent overview of the different catastrophic possibilities together with a way out of them is provided by *The Seventh Enemy* by Ronald Higgins (published by Hodder and Stoughton 1978).

There are many books which speculate on whether or not we are entering a new stage of development in society and what it will look like. A good overview of some different approaches is provided in the first part of Jonathan Gershuny's. *After Industrial Society?* (Macmillan 1978).

For a more colourful view, and a thought-provoking one, I recommend some 'social fiction', Kurt Vonnegnt's *Player Piano* (Panther 1975), which looks through the eyes of Rudi, a worker of sorts, in an automated society in which only the highly-educated have proper jobs, the rest living on pensions or make-work projects.

For a more positive view of the possibilities you should try J. Robertson's *A Sane Alternative* published by the author and obtainable from 9 New Road, Ironbridge, Shropshire TF8 7AU. This book begins to look at some of the questions raised in the section entitled *A Fair Society?*

The existence of a Third Age depends on the facts about our population, how long they live, how they live, and how they work. The annual publication by the Central Industrial Office of Information *Social Trends* (HMSO) makes surprisingly fascinating reading if you are interested in these things. It is expensive (the 1982 edition costs £19.95) but is available in libraries.

There are also one hundred and seventy universities of the Third Age in the world, which is in itself a powerful indication that the phenomenon does exist, and one has just been founded in England. For information write to the Secretary: Dianne Norton, University of the Third Age, 6 Parkside Gardens, London SW19

For a general overview of how the fifties fit into the whole picture of your life, I suggest the readable book by J. Nicholson, *Seven Ages* (Fontana 1980), or the American G. Sheehy's *Passages, The Predictable Crisis of Adult Life* (Dutton, New York, 1976) – both of which will suggest other reading in this general area.

A useful study done in Britain, most of which is relevant to our age-group, is M. P. Fogarty's *Forty to Sixty: How We Waste The Middle-Aged* (Bedford Square Press 1975).

CHAPTER TWO
WHAT WILL THE EIGHTIES BE LIKE?

The book which sets out most clearly the scenario of 'absolute automation' which I have developed in this chapter is B. Jordan's *Automatic Poverty* (Routledge & Kegan Paul 1981). Bill Jordan is a sociologist and economist and his book is serious reading, but important. It focuses entirely on the UK. Another book with a more global view point is R. Heilbronner's *Business Civilization in Decline* (Pelican 1977). These two books are both pessimistic about the future for the economies of the industrialised countries. For a more neutral and dispassionate view I can recommend the recent report of the Council for Science and Society published as a small paperback under the title *New Technology: Society, Employment and Skill* (Council for Science and Society 1981, 3/4 St Andrew's Hill, EC4V 5BY).

The informal economy has mainly been the subject of newspaper activities rather than books and these articles have mostly concentrated on the black economy, but the second half of Jonathan

Gershuny's book (listed under Chapter One) does deal with what he calls the 'emerging self-service economy'. A study of the important household economy in the USA is to be found in Scott Burns' *The Household Economy* (Beacon Press, Boston 1976).

There are many investigations going on in the EEC countries into the possible ways of shortening working time and of changing the three forty-eights. A recent British study of the question is reported in M. White's *Shorter Working Time* (Policy Studies Institute 1980). This study suggests that only a lowering of retirement age would have any effect on unemployment.

CHAPTER THREE

WORK OR WHAT?

The scope for different ways of working in organisations is well discussed, with lots of examples, in D. Clutterbuck and R. Hill, *The Re-Making of Work* (Grant McIntyre 1981).

Readable accounts of the 'Microprocessor revolution' are given in *The Mighty Micro* (Gollancz 1979) by a computer scientist, C. Evans, and C. Jenkins and B. Sherman, *The Collapse of Work* (Eyre Methven 1979) from a trade union viewpoint.

There is one article which deserves to be more widely read, if you can dig it out of the files, because it is very prophetic and provocative. It is N. Macrae's *The Coming Entrepreneurial Revolution*, published in *The Economist*, Christmas Day 1976. It's sequel *Intrapreneurial Now* was also published in *The Economist*, April 17 1982.

The whole question of what we work for in modern society is discussed in an important, but difficult, book: *Social Limits to Growth*, F. Hirsch (Routledge and Kegan Paul 1976). A good short description of the kind of work possibilities discussed in this chapter is provided in *The Redistribution of Work* available (price £1) from Turning Point, 9 New Road, Ironbridge, Shropshire, TF8 7AU. *The Turning Point Newsletter*, available from the same address, is a good inventory of new ideas and development in the general area of local initiatives.

A very useful and practical handbook for anyone who finds themselves unemployed is G. Dauncey's *The Unemployment Handbook* (National Extension College, 18 Brooklands Avenue, Cambridge); this book is full of ideas, people to contact and things to do.

Two other useful books are

Joy Melville's *The Survivor's Guide to Unemployment and Redundancy* (Corgi 1981) and Tony Lynes *The Penguin Guide to Supplementary Benefits* (Penguin 1981)

CHAPTER FOUR

TAKING STOCK OF YOURSELF

There are stacks of books which set out to help you to understand yourself. One to start with would be: A. G. Kirn and M. O. Kirn's *Life Work Planning* (McGraw-Hill Book Company 1978).

Managers and executives will find exercises relevant to their world neatly set out and described in M. Pedler, J. Burgoyne, T. Boydell, *A Manager's Guide to Self-Development* (McGraw-Hill 1978).

Women could find the chatty checklists useful in Shirley Conran and Elizabeth Sidney's *Futurewoman* (Penguin 1981).

Two books for women in their fifties with an interesting perspective, one British, one American, are H. Franks *The Prime Time* (Pan 1981) and L. Rubin *Women of a Certain Age* (Harper Colophon, New York 1979).

Men in their fifties have been a little neglected in the book lists, but one American study has many things of interest: D. J. Levinson, *The Seasons of a Man's Life* (Knopf, New York, 1978).

A fuller description of the Greek Gods as a way of thinking about personal styles of behaviour is to be found in C. Handy *Gods of Management* (Pan 1978).

A nice introduction to personality is H. J. Eysenck's *Know Your Own Personality* (Penguin 1976).

CHAPTER FIVE

NETWORKS

Relationships, particularly in marriage, is another subject that fills the bookshelves. A good place to start reading is J. Bernard *The Future of Marriage* (Penguin 1976), which I have found to be a good introduction albeit from an American viewpoint.

An excellent study of the marriages of busy men is to be found in P. Evans and F. Bartolome, *Must Success Cost So Much?* (Grant McIntyre 1980). This is a study of successful executives but the questions which it raises are surely applicable to all marriages.

A big, solid but useful book full of ideas and research is R. Rapoport and R. N. Rapoport, *Leisure and the Family Life-Cycle* (Routledge & Kegan Paul 1975).

CHAPTER SIX

FACING UP TO YOUR WORRIES

This is an area of very practical concerns. There are some useful handbooks, but inevitably they get out of date fairly quickly. Stress is a popular subject and a good book to start with is C. Cooper, *The Stress Check: Coping with Life and Work Stress* (Prentice Hall 1980).

Health is discussed in a general and informative way in S. Lock & T. Smith, *The Medical Risks of Life* (Penguin 1976), and in a very practical way in *The Time of Your Life, a handbook for retirement* (Help the Aged 1979) which is aimed at the over-sixties but is just as useful for the under-sixties.

A health book for women of all ages which has a chapter on menopause and a list of additional reading and resources is A. Phillips and J. Rakusen, *Our Bodies Ourselves* (Penguin 1979).

Dr. B. Wright's *Executive Ease and Disease* (Pan 1977) is full of practical advice.

A useful book on money is J. Allen, *Your Taxes and Savings in Retirement* (Age Concern 1981).

CHAPTER SEVEN
CHANGING

A classic book in this area is P. Marris, *Loss and Change* (Routledge and Kegan Paul 1974); it is serious reading, but important.

Women would be interested in B. Musgrave and Z. Menell, *Change and Choice, Women and Middle Age* (Peter Owen 1980).

Futurewoman by Shirley Conran and Elizabeth Sidney, also listed under Chapter 4, has many practical ideas to do with change. It is principally directed at the middle-aged woman.

CHAPTER EIGHT
THE QUESTIONS FOR SOCIETY

This chapter is concerned with social policy issues and there are obviously lots of books around, many with a political flavour. One of the more recent and lively of these is – S. Windass, *Politics thro' the Looking-Glass*, published by New Foundations, The Rookery, Adderbury Banbury OX17 3NA, which addresses many of the questions in this chapter. The foreword is written by Shirley Williams which gives an indication of its political flavour.

A recent, good, study of pension policy issues is M. P. Fogarty, *Retirement Age and Retirement Costs* (Policy Studies Institute 1980), but, inevitably, it does quickly get into technical detail.

The classic work on taxation, including discussion of a social wage, is the Report of the Meade Committee, *The Structure and Reform of Direct Taxation* (Allen & Unwin 1978) but here again, it is inevitably very technical. There are no simple discussions of these topics; perhaps there cannot be.